EastEnders

BIANCA'S
Secret Diary

D1346920

This book is published to accompany the BBC television series *EastEnders*.
Executive Producer: Matthew Robinson

Published by BBC Worldwide Ltd, Woodlands, 80 Wood Lane, London W12 0TT

First published 1999

ISBN 0 563 55162 3

Editorial Consultant: Art Young
Commissioning Editor: Emma Shackleton
Project Editor: Lara Speicher
Copy Editor: Barbara Nash
Book Design: Lisa Pettibone/Ann Ramsbottom
Picture Research: Ross Anderson
Script Research: Sharon Batten

Printed and bound in Great Britain by Redwood Books, Trowbridge, Wiltshire
Colour picture section printed by Lawrence Allen, Weston-super-Mare
Cover printed by Belmont Press Ltd, Northampton

Front cover photograph of
Bianca Butcher (Patsy Palmer): John Rogers
Stylist: Phil Tarling
Make-up: Jenny Ede-England
Shirt: Pilot
Necklace: Debenhams

EastEnders

BIANCA'S
Secret Diary

As seen by Kate Lock

1 January

Last night I saw my best friend die.

I thought that writing it down might help – you know, seeing it in black and white, 'Tiffany's dead'. Cos somehow, it still don't seem real.

Stupid, innit? I mean, I saw her with me own eyes. She was lying on the road in front of Frank's car and the first thing I thought was, why ain't she moving? Why doesn't she just get up? Then I got closer and I saw this dark puddle round her head. She sort of looked up at us all – everyone was crowding out of the Vic – and she tried to say something and then – then, I can't explain it. It was like a candle being blown out. The light just went out of her eyes. Someone called an ambulance and I sat, waiting for it to arrive, holding her cold little hand, praying for even the faintest squeeze. I kept telling meself, perhaps she's in a coma, like before when Grant pushed her down the stairs, but deep down I knew it was no good. The paramedics couldn't do nothing and when we got to the hospital this doctor came and told me she was dead.

When he said that, I just turned and ran out. It was the hospital where Natasha died and I kept getting these awful flashbacks, seeing her tiny body in that basket they brought her to me in. She looked just like a little doll. A stiff, still little baby doll. I started panicking about Liam then. I'd left Pat with him, but he's only a week old, barely out of hospital himself, and he was premature. I screamed at this taxi driver, 'I've got to get home, my baby needs me!' I was so scared something might have happened to him, too.

Course, Liam was fine, but I was going mental cos Ricky wasn't there. He went to the club earlier and he didn't come home all night. I didn't get a wink of sleep; I just sat there with all these questions going round my head, cuddling Liam and crying into his hair. Then, when Ricky did have the nerve to show his face at ten o'clock the next morning, it was obvious he'd only just heard about Tiff. He came stumbling through the door, hair all on end, looking like something the cat had dragged in. He said he'd got legless and crashed at the squat, but for once I didn't care. Normally, I'd have screamed at him but I just said, 'I hope it was worth it. I've been on my own all night. I really needed you.' He asked how it had happened and I told him Tiff was chasing after Grant and Frank knocked her down. Instead of comforting me, he went, 'How is he? Was he hurt?' It took my breath away. Tiffany's dead and he wants to know how Frank is! I said, 'I don't know. I didn't stop to ask how he was feeling!' I mean, his dad's alive, inni?

Truth is, I can't face seeing Frank any more than I can stomach seeing that animal Grant Mitchell. If Tiff hadn't been running after him and Courtney, she would never have dashed out into the road. But if Frank Butcher hadn't been driving round the corner, my best friend would still be alive. I don't know if I can ever forgive him for that. He came round to the flat today but I stayed in the bedroom until he'd gone.

After that I went round to see Beppe. He's the one bloke who stood by Tiffany and I know he really loved her. I thought he must be feeling as terrible as me, but his face was like a mask and I couldn't get through to him. I said, 'Why couldn't Tiff have left with you? Why did she have to change her mind?', cos she was gonna run off with him before. He said he couldn't help me and that was that. Practically shut the door on me.

Since then, I've just been sitting here, writing this and thinking about Tiff. Every time I hear the door slam downstairs, I expect her to come breezing in, all smiles, how she was. I know it ain't logical but I can't help it. She was here only last night. Her presence is still so strong. I can smell her perfume in the room. Her lipstick's on a glass in front of me. There's a black hair of hers on the cushion. How can she be dead?

She came to tell me she was leaving. Her and Courtney were going off to Spain to start a new life, away from Grant. We drank Champagne, had a laugh, talked about the old days – me and Tiff had some wild times together when we was teenagers – then she said she had to go. We hugged. Both of us was in tears. It was hard enough to get me head round the fact that she was going away to another country. I said, 'What am I gonna do without you?'

I didn't realize it would be forever.

5 January

I can't believe I've been so stupid. I've lost the letter Tiff gave me New Year's Eve. I've been turning the flat upside down trying to find it. Sonia's been helping me aswell, but it just seems to have vanished. I feel completely gutted. It was the last thing Tiffany ever gave me. She wanted me to hand it to the police after she'd gone to Spain. I said to her, 'It's about Grant, innit?' but she just went, 'It's better if you don't know'. I only remembered it this morning – I've been walking around like a zombie ever since she died. My eyes feel like they're about to fall out of my face, I've been crying so much. Just doing normal things, like getting dressed and eating and washing, has been a massive effort. If it weren't for Liam, I'd crawl under the duvet and stay there. He's exhausting but at least looking after him takes my mind off Tiff. That's why I totally forgot all about the letter.

Haven't been able to face setting the stall up, but then Simon ain't up to working, so there's no point anyway. He looks how I feel – terrible. We talked about the funeral, but it's out of our hands. Grant's next of kin. I said, 'Maybe his girlfriend can give him a hand; he can bring her out of hiding now.' Simon agrees, it's only a matter of time before Grant slips up and we'll catch him out. I'd love to know who the slut is, just so as I can tell her exactly what damage she's done. In a way, though, I almost pity her. If she knew what Grant put Tiff through, she wouldn't go near him.

Looking back, that's when everything went wrong. Before Tiff found out about Grant's affair, she was really happy. Next thing I knew, she was round our flat in floods of tears, packing her bags and trying to get away to Italy with Beppe. She told me Grant was having an affair, but she wouldn't say who with. If only she'd managed to escape then – but instead, Grant pushed her down the stairs and she landed up in hospital in a coma, while he was free to carry on with his fancy piece. The only thing that gives me any pleasure at all right now is the thought that Grant's gonna go down for what he did for a very long time.

I can hardly bear to go outside – the railings round the garden in the Square have got bunches of flowers piled up against them, loads of them. Ricky says it shows how much people loved her, but I wish they weren't there. All I can think of when I see them is Tiffany lying in the road with her hair soaked in blood.

I can't get the image of it out of my mind. It's giving me nightmares. I see her in my sleep, running out of the Vic after Grant, and I try and shout 'Stop!', but it comes out in a faint little whisper and she don't hear me. Then Frank's car comes round the corner and I hear Tiff scream … I keep waking up wringing wet, me heart going nineteen to the dozen. What with Liam waking us every two or three hours as well, I'm totally worn out.

I wish I had someone to talk to about all this, but there's no-one. Tiff was the person I told everything to. We've been there for each other since we was kids at school. I thought we'd carry on being friends 'til we was batty old ladies, like Dot and Ethel. We never thought either of us would die young – you just don't, do you? I know we had our fallings out, but they never lasted long. I miss her so much.

Even with Ricky, I can't tell him things like I used to tell things to Tiff. I mean, half of what I told her was about Ricky!

Anyway, he's flapping around Frank – which we ain't seeing eye-to-eye about – so things are a bit strained at the moment. Then there's me mum, but she's the other side of London and they've got their own worries, what with being in witness protection. I just feel so lonely.

I think I'm gonna carry on with this diary. There's all this stuff flying round my head and now I ain't got Tiff, it's somewhere I can say what's really on me mind. I ain't done one before, but I know Tiffany kept one. I rescued it from her luggage after she died and I've put it in a safe place, for Courtney. Me and Sonia have been talking and we decided we're gonna hang on to all our memories of the good times we had with Tiff so we can tell Courtney about them when she's older. Something else Sonia said, 'We'll make sure Liam and Courtney are friends. We won't let her forget.' It's the least we can do.

11 January

Frank came round the flat today. He said he wanted to see Liam, but I could tell that were just an excuse. He was in a right old state, blubbing all over the sofa. He went, 'You don't know what it means to me to be able to come here and talk to you.' I could feel meself getting more and more angry. Ricky's been all tea and sympathy with him – he is his dad after all – but it's no good Frank expecting that from me. I told him straight: I can't stand the sight of him. He went off with his tail between his legs.

Ricky went mad when he found out. Says his dad could crack any minute and the last time that happened he disappeared for two years. It made me feel guilty but I just couldn't help it. I've never been one for hiding what I think and I ain't gonna start now. It's Tiff's funeral tomorrow. She was supposed to be starting a new life, not lying dead in a coffin. And who's responsible for that?

12 January

It all makes sense now, Tiff saying she had to get away from Walford and being in such a hurry to leave. It all makes sense because I've got the truth from her own lips – or from her own pen, anyway. Sonia found the letter – it was at the bottom of the rubbish bin, folded up in a newspaper – and she brought it to me at the church. I didn't know 'til after the funeral, cos she got there late and had to sit at the back.

We had to sit through Grant Mitchell's little sermon first on how much he loved Tiffany and how no-one would ever understand what they had together and all that rubbish. When I think of how many times she turned up on my doorstep after he'd thumped her, it makes my blood boil. I know just what they had. At least Simon stood up to him. He got up at the pulpit and accused Grant of destroying her. You could hear this intake of breath go round the church, cos it was obvious Simon was losing it, but we all knew he was right.

Afterwards, everyone went out to go to the crematorium, which was when Sonia gave me the letter. I couldn't handle the thought of going there anyway, so I was glad of an excuse to stay behind. I just wanted to be on me own with Tiff – with my memories of her – but I still wasn't prepared for what she had to say. I've got the letter in my handbag now. This is it:

Dear B

I wish I could talk to you about this but I can't. You won't believe this, but the woman Grant was having an affair with was my mum. Now you know why I've got to get away. But there's one thing I've got to get straight before I go. Grant never pushed me down the stairs. I lied because I couldn't face a battle over Courtney, and because Beppe made me realize there was a way out of the situation. But I can't let Grant do time for something he never did. He is Courtney's dad, after all, and I did love him once. So could you please

*pass this letter to the police for me? Thanks a lot, B. And
don't worry about me, OK? I'm going to be fine. Take care.
I'll write soon, once we're settled in Spain.
Loads of love, Tiff*

So it was Louise all along. Tiff's own mother. The treacherous,
two-faced lying cow. She put on this big act of being supportive, taking Tiff in, telling her to leave Grant, to be strong – and
all because she wanted him for herself. I never rated her that
highly – she always carried on like a bit of a slapper – but
I never thought even Louise would stoop as low as this. To steal
her own daughter's husband! She saw how mixed up Tiff was.
Doesn't that woman have any morals? Tiff turned to her for
help, she trusted her, and all the time Louise was lying and
cheating and making a mockery of her marriage. Back-stabbing
bitch. I can't begin to imagine how betrayed Tiff must've felt.

Thinking about it made me realize what I had to do. I went
round the Vic, where they were having the wake. There was
music blaring out and people were dancing. I went over to
Louise and got her by the arm. I told her to get out of Walford
and that if she didn't, I'd tell Simon her dirty little secret and
then she'd lose her son as well as her daughter.

14 January

Louise was still here this morning. I saw her in the market
when I was setting up the stall. I just couldn't believe she had
the nerve to show her face again. I told her I meant what I'd
said, that I wanted her out. By the end of the day. She tried to
guilt-trip me, saying I'd take her away from Simon and that
would be going against what Tiff would've wanted, but I called
her bluff. I said, 'I reckon Tiffany would've been better off
telling Simon the truth. But she's dead now so I'm tying up the
loose ends.' Louise just gave me that constipated camel look of
hers and stalked off.

I saw her in the garden later, talking to Grant. I said, 'So what's this, then? The lovers' last meeting?' She gave me a right dirty look and waved a ticket folder at me and said, 'I'm going, OK?' She didn't say where and I don't care, so long as it's far away from Albert Square. I said, 'So what you waiting for, a farewell party?' and she said she was trying to work out what to say to Simon. I told her, try lying, you've had loads of practice. She started slagging me off so I gave her both barrels, face to face. I said, 'Some days I think Tiffany's better off dead, cos at least this way she don't have to have you as a mother no more.'

At least I gave her the chance to leave with some kind of dignity – not that she deserves it. If people knew the real reason, she'd be hounded out the Square. The only reason I'm not shouting her sordid little secret from the rooftops is because I don't want Simon to get hurt. Louise said, 'Do you know what it's going to do to Simon when he finds out I'm leaving?', but like I told her, it's nothing compared to how he'd be if he found out what she'd been up to.

All the same, it's eating me up, carrying this about. I needed to tell someone, to get it off my chest, so I let Ricky in on it this morning. He said I shouldn't get involved and to stay out of it, but that's Ricky for you. He always lets things ride. Me, I prefer to tackle them head on.

Take Frank. I've been feeling really bad about what I said to him. Poor old Frank, he's suffering so much, taking all the blame on himself. Grant's making him out to be the villain of the piece and Frank's just rolled over and accepted it. He's moved out of the Vic and things are really strained between him and Peggy. He didn't even come to the funeral. I know I was angry at him before, but I needed someone to pin Tiffany's death on. Now I know who's really to blame – Louise and Grant. Me and Ricky talked about it and we decided to ask Frank to be godfather to Liam to make up for it.

When I called at Frank's flat he came to the door looking like death warmed up. He wouldn't let me in – said the place was a tip – but I persuaded him to come with me and Liam to the park and feed the ducks. He turned me down at first when I asked him to be a godfather. Said he was a walking disaster area and he couldn't hold such a position of trust. I tried to convince him what happened to Tiffany wasn't his fault and he said I'd changed my tune, which made me feel even more rotten about mouthing off. I told him I was sorry and that I'd been out of order and I didn't want to lose his friendship. We both ended up hugging and I said, 'There you go – something else unusual. Bianca Butcher apologizing.' I know I can be difficult. (How did Frank put it? 'You have your moments.') I know I bawl people out. But at least I know when I'm in the wrong and I've got the guts to admit it. Unlike some other people around here.

18 January

It's two in the morning and I can't sleep. Liam's restless and I'm churning this letter business round and round in my head. Ricky gave me a right rollicking when he read it – he sneaked it out my handbag this afternoon – and said I should have given it to the police, like Tiffany wanted. If I'm honest, I've been ignoring that bit. As far as I'm concerned, Grant and Louise have got Tiff's blood on their hands. If Grant Mitchell gets life for his crime, it won't be long enough. He might not have pushed Tiffany down the stairs but he succeeded in killing her anyway, so what's the difference? It's just a pity they can't chuck Louise in with him and throw away the key. They could rot together.

Course, they'd have to find her first. She must've gone not long after I saw her in the Square the other day, cos there ain't been no sign of her since. Gianni said he saw her heading off to the Tube station with all her luggage. He said she was in tears. So she has got a heart after all, eh? Who'd've thought it? Certainly not me. I expect she was just feeling sorry for herself. After all, she's gotta slap on the warpaint and pinch someone else's husband now. Let's face it, she's forty. There ain't many blokes who go for her cheap brand of mutton dressed as lamb.

Ricky says I've got no right to play God and that Grant's an innocent man. I don't believe that, but there was one thing he said that keeps coming back to me: 'Are you going to go against Tiffany's final wish?' I know she wanted to put Grant in the clear, but she didn't know when she wrote that the price she was gonna have to pay. If I keep hold of the letter, Grant will get what he deserves. If I give it to the police, he's gonna get off scott-free yet again. So what do I do?

Trouble is, I always tend to act first and think later. That's why Ricky's so good for me, he balances me out. He's never gonna set the world on fire but he's steady, you can rely on him, whereas I just charge in like a bull in a china shop. I know he thinks I interfere too much – he guessed it was me sent Louise packing – but what was I expected to say to her? 'I hear you slept with Grant ... Never mind, it's all water under the bridge now your daughter's dead, innit?' I'll never forgive her for what she's done. Never. To betray your own like that – it's despicable.

I do feel bad about Simon, though. Even Ricky noticed he was acting strange. He's gone into overdrive on the stall, acting like nothing's happened. Tony's worried, too. He thinks Simon's gonna work himself into the ground. I ran into Tony in the caff and he said Louise going was the final straw. I said, 'We'll just have to keep a close eye on him, then, eh?' I'm sure me and Tony'll do more good for him than Louise would, anyway. I mean, what's the point of him relying on a mother like that? She's always disappearing, it's not as if that's anything new...

19 January

Oh God, it's just getting more and more tangled. I woke up vowing to do the right thing by Tiff and give the letter to the police, but then I saw Simon in the market and he said the only thing keeping him going was the thought of Grant going down. What if this tips him over the edge? Thing is, Ricky's right – I can't go against what Tiffany asked me to do. What kind of a friend would that make me?

I did try to call the station. I got as far as asking for that detective Mason bloke but then I chickened out and put the phone down. I was hoping Ricky might've forgotten about it – fat chance, I know – but of course he hadn't. He asked me this evening if I'd done it and I had to confess I couldn't go through with it cos of Simon. Ricky thinks we should ask Simon to be Liam's other godfather and hopefully that'll cheer him up, but I'm not convinced. He's becoming obsessed with Grant.

Anyway, then I had this bright idea. I thought, well, Beppe's a policeman, ain't he? He cared about Tiff. (I still can't work out why she didn't go off with him. He's so kind, and he's gorgeous. I'd be tempted.) If anyone's got a right to it, he has. So I went out there and then – it was gone ten, but I just wanted to get it over and done with – and found him walking home from the Vic. I shoved the letter into his hand and said, 'Tiff gave me this on New Year's Eve. She wanted me to give it to the police after she'd left. I've done my bit. Now it's up to you.'

21 January

Me and Ricky seem to be drifting along in a haze of tiredness. I used to think nights was for sleeping. Now I'm up two, three times with Liam, sometimes more – he seems to cry constantly. Just as I sink back into sleep, it's shattered by this piercing yell and off he goes again. What with that and worrying about whether I'd done the right thing giving the letter to Beppe, I hardly got a wink last night.

I keep wondering whether there's something wrong with Liam. I mean, how can you tell? I always assume he's hungry or wet or tired, but maybe there's something else going on. I ran into Ruth at the launderette and asked her – after all, she works with kids – and she said it was normal for babies to scream for ages and then go really quiet. All the same, I might get the Health Visitor to check him over. Can't hurt, can it?

Sonia's been really good, helping out with Liam and around the home. Honestly, she's a different girl, keen to do the chores and everything. Plus, Liam really likes her – she can get him to stop crying when I can't. She says it's because I'm too uptight and babies can sense tension. Just wish she'd stop banging on about the Christening, though, as if I haven't got enough on me plate. Talking of which, I asked Simon about being the other godfather and he agreed, although he was a bit suspicious at first and said I was just doing it to try and cheer him up. I went, 'Nooo, course not.' Trouble with being a redhead is, you blush so easy!

10.30 p.m: This thing with the letter is spiralling out of control. First off, Beppe came round the flat this evening, telling me not to spread the word about the letter. I said I hadn't – which isn't quite true, but then Ricky don't count – and he said, 'Good, so let's just keep it just between us, then, yeah?' and shot off again. I can only take that one way – he ain't gonna hand it in – which is fine by me, my conscience is clear.

Fifteen minutes later there's another ring on the doorbell and Grant appears. He'd brought over some of Courtney's baby clothes for Liam, but I could tell that was just an excuse. I went, 'So. What do you really want?' and then he started to try and pump me about Tiff, asking if she'd told me anything that would help his case. As if I'm gonna give him that! I kept me mouth shut and he got more and more angry and started yelling and then Ricky burst in and told him to back off. Course I know Ricky was just trying to defend me, but he landed me right in it, telling Grant he should be thanking me cos I'd done the decent thing about the letter. Grant goes, 'What letter?' and his eyes were bulging and I knew he'd shake it out of me if I didn't say summat. I said, 'Ask Beppe, he's got it now. It puts you in the clear.' He went storming off to find him and I've been sitting here with me stomach tied in knots ever since. It's even affecting my milk. When I think about that maniac I just want to punch his lights out. It can't be good for Liam, me carrying around all this hate. No wonder the poor little lamb's crying so much. I think we're in for another sleepless night.

22 January

Plucked up courage to go and see Beppe this afternoon and apologize for Ricky blurting out about the letter. I thought he'd be mad at us but he was OK about it really. A bit distant, but that's all. No bruises, I was glad to see, and the door seemed to have survived intact, too. I said, 'So what have you done with it? Handed it in?' cos I guess he don't have any option now. He didn't reply, just said he was in a hurry and had to go somewhere. He had a suit and tie on, so it must've been something important.

Ricky and I have decided to make Sonia Liam's godmother. She's been dropping so many hints and she is brilliant with him. Even changes his nappy! I know she's a bit young, but she's very responsible, and what with being cut off from the rest of the family, it's the least I can do. I know she misses Billy and Mum and Alan. This way she gets a little bit of family back. And we get a willing babysitter!

26 January

It's the inquest into Tiffany's death today. I couldn't face hearing all the gory details being read out – I've only just stopped getting those nightmares – so I didn't go in the end. Neither did Ricky, though he wanted to be there, to support his dad. Frank didn't want him there, though. He said he needed to be alone, or he'd never be able to hold it together. It's hard for Ricky, but I'm relieved. I'd much rather have him here with me.

Feeling very low today. It's like this is the final chapter. After this, people will draw a line under things and that will be Tiffany disposed of, forgotten about. I'm determined that ain't gonna happen.

27 January

The inquest verdict was accidental death. Ricky's pleased of course – it proves Frank's innocent – but I'm with Simon and Tony: it should have been something that put the blame on Grant. He as good as murdered her. I always had this feeling that one day he'd kill her, the way he beat her up and bullied her and betrayed her. I lost count of the number of times she left him and each time I warned her not to go back. I told her he was dangerous, but she was convinced she was the only one who really understood him. Only she didn't, did she? And he got her in the end. Not with his fists, but the result's the same.

But that ain't the end of it. The CPS has dropped the charges against Grant. I heard it from Tony this morning. I found him running my stall – he'd sent Simon home because he was in such a state – and he said Grant was going around telling anyone who would listen. Something about they couldn't bring a case against him because Tiffany couldn't be cross-examined. Well, isn't that the point??? The man's a monster! From what Tony said, people weren't that impressed. They still think Grant did it, it's just that there's no proof. He didn't mention anything about Tiff's letter. I can't work it out. I suppose Beppe must've hung on to it, after all.

1 February

Beppe didn't keep the letter. He burnt it. He said he didn't want Grant to get away with what he'd done. He told me today – he's been suspended. He said I might get a visit from his boss. Ricky gave me a hard time over it. He said, 'You knew Beppe wouldn't hand it over, didn't you?' I suppose I did, really. It seemed the obvious way out: do what Tiffany wanted without letting Grant off the hook. Only now I've gone and landed meself in more trouble.

8 February

God, I'm knackered. I don't know how these career women do it, juggling work and having kids. Simon called in sick so I've been running the stall all day (I can't leave it with Tony, he hasn't got a clue). Pat and Frank have taken it in turns to mind Liam, but I feel awful about deserting him for so long and I missed him like crazy. I kept worrying he might forget who his mum was, or think I don't care or something. Frank asked me what I was gonna do, long term – keep the stall or stay at home with Liam – but the truth is, I don't know. I mean, Simon was only ever supposed to be temporary cover. And I've put everything into that stall. I don't want it to stop there. I still want a shop eventually. But I feel so torn. I can't bear the thought of not being with Liam. Trouble is, I haven't had a chance to think it through. What with everything that's happened since Liam was born I've just been living from day to day. Ricky ain't too keen on me working, cos he's seen how tired I am, but I don't have much choice at the moment, do I?

Got a visit from some nosy cow policewoman this morning. She gave me a right grilling about why I didn't hand the letter in straight away and why I gave it to Beppe instead. I was a bit worried for a moment, the way she was going on, but I stuck to my guns and in the end she said I'd been very helpful. Can't think why. I wasn't trying to be.

14 February

I remember when Valentine's Day meant dressing up and bein' wined and dined by candlelight. Seems a lifetime ago. Babies don't do much for romance, I can tell you. And as for getting dolled up – forget it. What's the point of putting on something nice, only to have Liam chuck up baby sick all over it? Anyways, me and Ricky haven't got the energy to go out partying – unlike half the Square, we're giving the opening night at the club a miss. These days I'm happy just to put me feet up for an hour and veg out in front of the telly. Ricky gave me flowers and chocolates, which was really sweet of him. We rented a video, *Sleepless in Seattle* (felt I could relate to the title) but only saw half of it – Liam woke up crying and it took me ages to get him to settle again.

15 February

Simon's still not shown his face. Tony's helping me on the stall but it's almost more hassle than it's worth cos I have to tell him how to do everything. He said he saw Simon yesterday and he was in a bad way. He was going on about calling the doctor, but I said I didn't think it was worth it. Simon's a bit depressed, but he ain't suicidal or nothing. Just wish he'd get himself sorted and get back to work on the stall. I don't know how much longer I can go on like this. I'm being as patient as I can, but there is a limit.

16 February

I thought doctors were supposed to be there to help when you got ill. Not our new doctor, oh no. I've been worried about Liam all day – he was snuffly this morning and he's been crying more than usual – but when I rang the surgery all I got was, 'We don't have any appointments left, bring him in tomorrow.' I said I only lived next door but the receptionist just repeated it like a broken record. I went, 'Well, in future I'll make an appointment before he gets ill, shall I?' cos I was so hacked off. I told her, Dr Legg was never like that.

I didn't take Liam out in his sling like I normally do, I kept him wrapped up indoors and we whacked the central heating up. At first, we thought it was just a cold. I've been taking him out on the stall with me, which I felt bad enough about as it was, thinking he'd got chilled, but by the evening he'd developed this red rash all over his face and he just wouldn't stop screaming. That was when Ricky rang Dr Fonseca and insisted he come round.

We was on the verge of calling an ambulance by the time he got here, we was so worried. I know about meningitis and Liam had some of the symptoms and it's not always easy to tell – look at what happened to Ben. Kathy only just got him to hospital in the nick of time. And doctors don't always get it right – you read these horror stories. Kid comes in, doctor says it's a throat infection, several hours later they're dead from meningitis. It's every parent's worst nightmare.

Not that we got any sympathy from this new bloke. He said Liam just had a cold and he was hot because the room was too warm. We said what about the rash, and he said it's natural for babies to cry and hadn't we heard the saying about them doing it 'til they're red in the face? Then he started going on about if he was called out every time a baby cried he wouldn't have time for his other cases, implying that we'd dragged him out for nothing.

I was really pissed off with him, and so was Ricky. It's all very well him thinking we're neurotic new parents, but we gotta reason for it, ain't we? We've already lost one little girl. I spent the whole pregnancy worrying about whether he'd have spina bifida and hydrocephalus like Natasha, and then when he was born it was such a huge relief we'd got through all of that and Liam was OK. He's so precious. I just couldn't bear it if anything happened to him, I just couldn't.

17 February

All change at the Vic. Frank's moved back in and Grant's moved out to Phil's, taking Courtney with him. Reading between the lines, I think Grant forced Peggy to make a choice and she chose Frank. It's about time she stood up to that son of hers. She's always running around after him and she gets no thanks from Grant. He's just a big sulky overgrown mummy's boy. Frank's over the moon of course, and Ricky's chuffed cos his dad's happy again. Apparently Peggy's going into overdrive on the wedding preparations, so sounds as if that's all back on track again.

I ain't sure about having her as a mother-in-law, though. Me and Peggy ain't exactly the best of friends at the moment. I put her back up when I let the whole of the Vic know her precious Grant was having an affair while his wife was lying in a hospital bed. It's been like Siberia between us ever since. We used to get on all right. Basically, I've always respected Peggy – she speaks her mind, same as I do, and she's straight up. She didn't stand for that George Palmer when she found out what he was really up to. If she's on your side, she's OK. But if she ain't, she's hell to play with.

Tiff found that one out. They had some rocky times, those two, but Peggy ended up batting for her in the end. The last time I saw Tiff, she said the only one of the Mitchells she'd miss was Peggy. She said Peggy was more of a mother to her than Louise had ever been. I know why, now. It's weird, thinking about it, me becoming Peggy's daughter-in-law. If things had turned out different, me and Tiff would've ended up related. I always felt she was like a sister to me. But she actually would've been, by marriage.

2 March

It's been a while, innit, but I've been rushed off me feet. It's all I can do to stay awake in the evenings, never mind write a bloomin' diary. Simon didn't come back on the stall until today and even he didn't appear 'til halfway through the morning. I said to Ricky, it's about time Simon joined the real world again. He can't mope around behind closed curtains for ever. As it turned out, he was in a really breezy mood. He said he'd just had some good news. I went, 'That makes a change round here', and then he said, 'Yeah, I've just had a phone call from Mum. She's coming back to the Square.'!!! I was speechless, and it takes a lot for that to happen. What the hell does that cow Louise think she's playing at? I thought she'd got the message. She knows she ain't welcome here and I told her what I'd do if she showed her face again. Tony goes, 'That's good, Simon needs all the good news he can get right now', and I'm thinking, what does he know? Ricky says I've got to think of Simon, but what he don't realize is, I *am* thinking of Simon…

Oh, and there's another major hassle. Someone's gone ahead and booked the Christening for a week on Wednesday. I only found out cos Nina said Peggy had okayed it with her and was organizing the caterers. I thought it was Ricky going behind me back, but he swears it ain't, so I don't know who's responsible. I suppose it could be Frank, he is a godfather, but I don't like having things like this sprung on me. It's my baby's Christening and I'll arrange it, thank you very much.

4 March

I waited outside Louise's flat this morning, trying to catch her the moment she arrived. Simon said she was coming first thing, so I told Ricky I was going shopping and nipped out with Liam after breakfast. Stupidly, I left my purse behind, so Ricky guessed what I was up to. I didn't say nothing cos I know he don't want me interfering, but me and Louise have unfinished business. As it turned out, there was no point Ricky doing his guardian angel stunt anyway, cos Simon got to Louise before I did and I could see he was really happy, so I just walked on by.

At least I found out who was behind the Christening idea. I cornered Robbie and he told me that it was Sonia. Then he went and told her I was on the warpath so she confessed. She came in to the launderette and went, 'Look, I know I'm in trouble. So go on, start shouting', as if I was gonna give her hell. She was going on about wanting to be a good god-mother and take the strain off me because I've been through so much, and how she'd got it all sorted, like the guests and the grub and what the vicar has to say an' all. When she finally drew breath, I said, 'Sonia, I'm really touched', and I meant it. She amazes me sometimes. Like I said to her, 'When I think about some of the families round here, it's good that we look out for each other.' No prizes for guessing which families were on my mind.

Talk of the devil, Louise herself turned up on my doorstep later on. I couldn't believe it. I said, 'You've got a nerve, show-ing your face around here,' and she said she wasn't gonna run away again, she's come back to look after Simon. 'Lucky boy,' I said, and she did that pouty thing and went, 'No, he's not been too lucky'. As if I need telling that! He ain't worked for two months! I said, 'No, I know, especially not in his choice of mother.' She said it didn't matter what I said, it couldn't make her feel worse about herself than she does already, which I find hard to believe. She's come back even more tarty looking with her hair dyed blonde. At her age!

I said, 'Well, what are you chasing after me for? What do you think we're gonna do? Kiss and make up?' and she kept on that she just wanted to do the best for Simon. 'Well, you can do that by leaving,' I said, 'cos I mean if Simon finds out what happened…' I don't think she's gonna be told, though, not this time. She had a different look about her, steely. She put the ball back in my court, saying that Simon was ill and anything could tip him over the edge and was I going to be the one to do it?' To be honest, I don't know…

God, what a couple of days! Yesterday mum phoned to say Alan had been taken to hospital. She was really upset and I was in a right panic because that was all we knew and it sounded really bad. Phil lent Ricky the Jag and we drove over there last night with Liam. He screamed for the first five minutes cos his routine was up the Swanney, but then he fell asleep, thank goodness.

The doctors thought Alan had had a heart attack at first, cos he'd had these pains in his chest and he keeled over, but now they think it was some stress-related thing, like a bad panic attack. It didn't sound like Alan – he's normally pretty laid back, but I suppose you never know with people.

We didn't get home 'til midnight, so I've been fit for nothing all day, then Mum rang up this afternoon and says she's got something to tell us ... it's over between her and Alan. So that was why he was in a state! I thought she was looking a bit weird yesterday, but I didn't twig what it was. Sonia was devastated, she's been going back there every weekend and she ain't noticed anything. I felt gutted, too. After all Mum and Alan have been through. They survived Frankie, they survived David, they held it together when Billy was kidnapped and then moving away from Walford and going into witness protection. I mean, those two aren't quitters. What's going on? I might go over there for a while, help Mum with Billy, try and find out the story.

Midnight. Again. Just wanted to update this. Simon came round tonight and said would it be all right if Louise came to the Christening? I was put on the spot, cos he's already asked her, and Ricky was giving me the eye, going, 'She can't do any harm, can she?' (Answer: Yes she can and she has, Ricky, though of course I couldn't say that in front of Simon.) After Simon had gone I went straight round to Louise's to ask her what she was playing at, but she said it was his idea. She said,

'He loves me and I've got a second chance with him and you're not going to ruin that', and I said, 'Well, if you love him so much, why don't you try telling him the truth? Tell him the real reason why you left and what you did to Tiffany.' I was gobsmacked when she said she'd been trying to and she would when Simon could handle it. Bet she don't. She's too much of a coward.

10 March

Today was Liam's Christening. The service went really well, although Robbie nearly stuffed things up. He arrived really late wearing this baggy suit he'd borrowed from Barry. I suppose I should've been grateful, he'd threatened to come in jeans. The words Alex said were lovely. He said he wanted us all to consider the precious gift of life that Liam represented. And it did make me think, cos I remembered how, when I was grieving for Natasha, Alex came and talked to me and it really helped. I ain't really a church-goer, except at Christmas and such, but I've gotta say that for a vicar, he ain't bad.

Liam was a perfect little angel all the way through the baptism, bless him. Afterwards, Mark took photos outside the church and we did family line-ups and all that stuff. I was glad to see Louise standing well out the way. I had to bite my lip to stop myself going for her, cos I really thought she was taking the mick, coming to the Christening and joining in with prayers for families, but Simon looked so happy and I didn't want to ruin Liam's day.

Afterwards we went back to the Vic for the reception and Ricky even made a half-decent speech. He said he wanted to drink a toast to his beautiful wife and wonderful baby, which was really sweet of him. I was having a good time until I discovered something he had been holding back from me. Like, we're gonna be homeless in a couple of weeks' time. Just a little detail really, as far as Ricky's concerned, obviously.

Otherwise I suppose he would have mentioned it in passing. I only found out because Lenny asked me where we were gonna live when we got evicted. He said the landlord's doing up the flats to sell them and we'd had a notice to quit.

I was so disgusted with Ricky for not saying anything that I walked out of the Vic and got mine and Liam's stuff packed up, bunged it all in a taxi and went over to Mum's. That's where I am now and I'm staying put until Ricky sorts us out somewhere else to live. I was gonna go for a bit anyway, we'd agreed that, but I didn't bother to tell him I was off and he was so busy nattering he didn't even notice.

Poor little Liam, what a way to start off in life. At the Christening, Alex talked about the journey Liam was about to embark on but I didn't plan on it being quite this quick. Or to Balham, for that matter. I could kill Ricky for doing this to us, I really could.

14 March

Things are awful here. Alan's still in hospital, having tests, Mum's spaced out and Billy's whinging and miserable. I'm still steaming about Ricky. He came over today, he's gonna spend weekends here, but we ended up having a huge row about the eviction notice. He said he was gonna tell me about it when he found the right moment. I said, 'And when would that be, Ricky? When we're sitting on the pavement with Liam surrounded by all our stuff?'

He makes me so mad, sometimes. I know he means well, but he always seems to stuff things up. That's what makes Ricky Ricky, I suppose. When I first met him I thought it was kind of cute, he can be so clueless, it's almost appealing, in a little-boy-lost sort of way, but now it drives me up the wall. To be honest, it's nice to have some space during the week. It's probably just what we need. Everything Ricky does these days seems to put my back up.

It's good to spend some time with me mum, too. I've hardly seen her since they left Walford, and that was all so sudden and so scary, what with Billy being kidnapped and Mum having to make an appeal on TV and the police camping out in our house. The blokes got done for the robbery and they're banged up now, but it still sends a shiver down my spine when I think about it.

Not that Mum ever lets on she's frightened, but she's very protective of Billy. So is Alan. I don't know what'll happen with Billy if they split up permanently. He's my little brother, I don't want to lose him. I don't want to lose Alan, either. I know he ain't my real dad, but it's always felt like he was. He's always been there for me, not like David. David wasn't around when I was growing up and he ain't around now. All I get from him is the odd postcard and, if I'm lucky, a birthday present two weeks late. I don't know where he's living now. He don't even know he's got a grandson.

It's gonna be really hard for Robbie and Sonia, too. We've all got different dads, but Alan's been around the longest, the others have just been and gone, and they were all a waste of space. Robbie's dad, Gary, was some sort of pervert into under-age sex. He ran off with a teenage girl and so Mum hooked up with Sonia's dad, Terry, who beat her and Robbie up. Mum don't talk about either of them, she just says Robbie and Sonia are better off without them. Alan moved in when Robbie was about nine and Sonia was two or three, so it's no wonder Sonia's upset. She worships the ground Alan walks on.

Mum and Alan just can't give up this easily. They've got to give it another go, for all our sakes.

16 March

Just heard from Ricky that Simon found out about Louise and Grant – apparently, she told him herself – and he went off the rails and set Louise's flat on fire. With himself inside! They only just got him out in time. He's got bad burns to his legs but he's going to be OK.

Ricky didn't know whether Simon did it deliberately or not. He said Simon was really upset when he found out. It was at the Christening reception, after I'd gone. One minute Simon was looking really happy, then when Ricky saw him again Simon was as white as a sheet and said, 'My mum's told me'. He was angry with me for not telling him about Grant and Louise, but I don't see how I'm to blame. I was trying to protect him. I thought about telling him often enough, I *wanted* to, but Louise said it would destroy him and Simon was so fragile that I just couldn't bring myself to do it.

Let's face it, there's only one person who can carry the can for poor old Simon's mental state, and that's Louise. The woman's pure poison. She's ripped her family apart with her selfish behaviour and now she's paid the price. Or rather, they have. The ultimate price, in Tiff's case. And now Simon's badly injured. What did they ever do to deserve a mother like that? Only love her. I hope she's in torment for the rest of her days.

17 March

It's hard work coping with Liam on my own, but Mum's been really supportive. It's funny how she just has that mother's knack of how to hold him and soothe him. He quietens instantly for her. Still, suppose she has had a lot of practice. I can't imagine bringing up four kids by myself, or coping with a baby at fifteen. That's how old she was when she had me – although she nearly didn't have me, cos David stumped up the cash for an abortion. Still freaks me out to think my own father paid to have me got rid of.

I know I had a termination with Natasha, but that was different. Her condition was so bad her life wouldn't have been worth living. Even so, I wouldn't do it again. No-one could understand it when I refused a scan with Liam, especially Pat –

we had a right falling out over it – but I knew I was gonna have him, whatever. I still feel guilty about Natasha, even though it was the sensible thing. That's what all the doctors said, but it don't make living with what you've done any easier. She'll always be with me, my little girl. She'll always be a part of our family. When Liam's older, we'll tell him about his sister.

23 March

Alan's home, recuperating. He looks really thin and drawn, like he's aged about twenty years. He's on some pills and has to go and see a stress counsellor and they've signed him off work for a month. He's supposed to be taking it easy and not getting worked up. Fat chance! It's like refereeing a boxing match with them two. All they do is fight about whose fault everything is. Alan's really stressed – I can see why he got sick – but Mum just freezes him out and refuses to talk things over. She's so stubborn, she won't even listen to him; either that or she turns round and gives him an earful. Sometimes, when I hear the way she goes for him, I wonder how he's stuck it as long as he has.

I had a long talk with Alan today about what went wrong between him and Mum. He said he's always known in the back of his mind that Mum was never really committed to him. She was always looking to be swept off her feet, but when her feet touched the ground again she got bored.

In a way, I can relate to that. When me and Ricky first got together both our families were dead against it, so we pretended nothing was going on. All the time we was sneaking around having these secret meetings in the park or in the Arches or in each other's houses when everybody was out. We even did it in the Portakabin once! It was exciting and danger-ous and romantic, and I thought I was head over heels in love. But passion, it don't last. We got the bedsit and settled down and suddenly things became domesticated and boring and I started thinking Ricky was acting middle-aged and dull.

I'll admit, there have been times when I wondered why I ever married him. We've had a pretty up-and-down history and I've left him a few times. We even split up while I was pregnant with Liam, after I found out he'd been involved in Christmas-tree rustling. He said he was doing it for me, to pay for my shop, but I told him I didn't want nothing to do with his ill-gotten gains. Ricky's been in trouble with the law once before over some dodgy cars of Phil's he was stupid enough to agree to work on. That time he got off with doing community service. Next time he mightn't be so lucky. I didn't want my baby growing up with his daddy in jail.

Anyway, that wasn't why I left Ricky, that time. The main point is trust. If you can't trust the person you're married to, then there ain't no point in being with them, as far as I'm concerned. Having said that, I've always come back to him again. I suppose it's because Ricky's a safe bet. Before him, I'd had these dodgy relationships with older men and I always ended up getting hurt, big time.

Not that Ricky's a saint. There was the time I caught him with that scheming cow Natalie and, even after we got back together, he started mooning around after Sam. I'll never forget seeing them kissing outside that club in Camden. That was when I chucked all his stuff out in the street and set fire to it. I kind of got my own back by sleeping with Lenny. It was just the once and I really regretted it afterwards – in fact, that was what made me decide to marry Ricky after all! I don't think Ricky'd look at another woman now. He wouldn't dare! But I can't be totally sure, can I? I thought Ricky was having an affair after we got married cos he kept disappearing. OK, so I was wrong, he was doing this speedway lark, which was pretty cool (and I didn't half fancy him in his leathers!), but you just never know with people. Look at Mum. She was carrying on with David behind Alan's back. Alan was just as bad, he went off with that singer, Frankie. As for poor Tiff, Grant flaunted his affair with Lorraine right under her nose. And then there was Louise. That one's the worst. Talk about doing the dirty on your own doorstep. I don't know how that woman can live with herself.

26 March

I want Mum and Alan to have marriage guidance counselling. Alan seems keen but Mum's refusing to even give it a try. I don't know what's going on with her, she won't open up at all, just says it's over between them. I even asked if she had someone else, but she said no. We had a big row about it and I told her she was being completely selfish. She said, 'Well, you'd know all about that, wouldn't you?' and I screamed back, 'If I'm selfish, it's because I've been following your example!'

Truth is, I have a real fear of ending up like my mum. Like mother, like daughter, that's what they say, innit? She's got a string of children from a string of crap relationships, she's never had a career and she ain't qualified to do nothing. I don't want to end up slaving away over someone else's laundry every day. That's why making a go of the stall is so important to me. I've got Tony looking after it while Simon's in the burns unit, but when I get back I'm gonna sort it out, get some new lines in, become more directional. I ain't given up on my dream for a shop, either. Just don't know how I'm gonna work it all, at the moment, what with Liam to look after too. But other women manage, don't they? Most mums work these days. I'll sort something out.

29 March

Ricky rang last night. He said Frank's come up with the perfect solution to our problem – we can move in to the Vic. I said, 'Are you off your head? You think I'm gonna let Peggy Butcher order me around?' but he said Peggy wouldn't be like that. Then he told me Peggy had breast cancer again and she's had

28

to have a mastectomy and I felt really awful, especially when he said Frank had found her cutting up her clothes.

Even if I could hack living with me in-laws – which would be hard enough, I mean, for starters we'll never have any privacy – the Vic's got too many bad memories for me. I can't be in that flat upstairs without thinking of Tiff, and Grant. It would give me nightmares all over again. But Ricky says he's been looking at other places and there's nothing within our price range. I've told him he'll just have to keep looking. There must be something. We're not *that* desperate.

1 April

April Fool's Day. Frank and Peggy are taking a chance, ain't they, getting married today? Ricky's best man but I'm not going. I said I was needed here. It's true, anyway. Mum and Alan have gone out for a walk – Alan's supposed to take regular gentle exercise – and I'm minding Billy. I think they're actually making an effort to get on, at last.

2 April

Ricky rang last night, pissed. He said the wedding went off well in the end, though Peggy cut it fine and Frank started to tell everyone the whole thing was off. I couldn't make out everything he was saying, because he was ringing from the Vic and it was really noisy, plus he was slurring his words. Something about him picking up the wrong suit and looking a total prat because the trousers were too short. Oh yeah, and he booked the wrong flight for Frank and Peggy so they'd had to leave early and missed their own reception. He kept going, 'I'm useless without you. I really love you, Bianca. Have I told you that? I really love you.'

He always gets like that when he's drunk.

4 April

Easter Sunday. Ricky, Sonia and Robbie were all here today. It was really nice, just like old times. Mum and Alan seemed quite happy and for once nobody argued. Felt like a proper family again. It was good to have Ricky here, too. I'm starting to miss him during the week and by the weekend we're both as randy as rabbits. I left Sonia minding Liam and dragged Ricky straight upstairs. You know what they say about absence making the heart grow fonder. Well, it's true!

6 April

Mum and Alan are giving it another go! I rang Sonia and she was so excited she was screaming, 'Yes, yes, yes!' down the phone. They've decided to try and spend some time together and go off and do things, so I'm holding the fort with Billy and Liam. It's not too bad, cos Billy goes to school and I've made friends with a couple of other girls down the road who've both got babies. Least it's people to go for a coffee and a natter with. This morning we took the little ones to the swimming pool – they've got this Water Babies class – and Liam had a splash around. I was terrified of him slipping out of my hands but he wasn't scared at all, he loved it.

I'm really enjoying this. It's the first chance I've had to relax and just spend time with Liam since he was born. Ricky's coming over at the weekend and we're going to do something all together. I'm looking forward to seeing him, but I'm in no hurry to get back to Albert Square. Just as well, cos Ricky's had no joy finding us anywhere to live apart from the Vic.

12 April

Went out for a drink last night with Karen, one of the girls I've got friendly with. It was fun to put on a bit of slap again and dress up a bit. Seems a long time since I did that. We only went down the local but it still felt like a big night out. Tragic, ain't it? Got a few looks, so I ain't past it yet. These two blokes bought us drinks and tried to chat us up, but we gave them the push (out of your league, boys). Still, it was nice to get the attention.

I remember when me and Tiff used to do that, dress up to the nines and tart about, getting men to buy us drinks. With make-up on we could pass for eighteen, even though we was only fifteen. We'd go and sit at the bar in these swanky hotels and the blokes would come swarming round, offering to buy us Champagne, cocktails, whatever we wanted. That's when Tiff started to get a bit of a reputation. Suppose I was in danger of it, too. We both thought if we could land a rich older man it would be our ticket out of the East End. Some hope, eh? All they ever did was take what they wanted, make a load of promises, then scarper.

There was one I really liked. He was married, but I didn't care about that. We had this mind-blowing affair, loads of passionate sex, but when he found out how old I was, you couldn't see his heels for dust. He meant the world to me and I was really cut up about it for ages afterwards. I thought I was in love with him, but what did I know? I'm older and wiser now.

Then we moved to Albert Square and I started seeing Richard, that market inspector (Tricky Dicky I later found out they called him). We slept together twice, then he told me it was finished, so me and Natalie got back at him by buying all these things on his credit card and putting it over the limit. He said he'd report us to the police, but I called his bluff, saying I'd report him for underage sex. It was a bit of a lie, cos I was actually sixteen, but he didn't know that, the slimy pervert. He kept his mouth shut.

I even made a pass at me own dad, which I squirm to think about, though I didn't know David Wicks was my father then. He'd come into the Square, all laid-back good looks, and I thought he was really tasty. To start with, he did flirt with me, which is a bit creepy when you think about it, both of us fancying each other, but then he didn't know either at that stage. Then he found out I was his daughter and would hardly give me the time of day.

No-one told me, though, did they? I just thought he'd gone off me. I thought, well stuff him, and that's when me and Ricky got together. It was only later, after me and Ricky split up over Natalie, that I found out the truth. I was drunk and upset and I wanted David to kiss me and when he wouldn't it was like the last straw. I thought I must be so hideous and unattractive that no-one wanted me, then he said it wasn't that, it was because he was my father!!!

It turned my world upside down completely. I mean, you can't help who you find attractive, can you? It's chemical. David and me, there was always a bit of a buzz between us. I mean, he never exactly acted fatherly towards me, even when he knew. And there I'd been, having fantasies about him. It was like, snap, you've got to switch that off. I felt disgusted with myself when I found out. Guilty, too. And angry, really angry at Mum for not saying nothing all this time. I mean she was watching us, she knew. And so did Pat.

It still makes me shudder, just thinking about it. What if David hadn't stopped me? What if he'd taken advantage? He was always chasing women. Luckily, he showed some principles for once and we came out of it OK in the end, but I was an emotional wreck for a while. When I found out about David and Mum getting together again, I was well confused. I didn't know whether to feel jealous, angry or glad. I mean, they are my real Mum and Dad...

13 April
Got a call from Tony today. He's leaving Walford to go travelling round Europe. I think Simon might have something to do with his decision, but he was really abrupt when I asked, just

32

said Si's better but he didn't know when he would be ready to take over the stall again. I've arranged for a temp to cover until Simon's back on his feet.

15 April

All change again. Simon's going with Tony! Glad they got there in the end. You could see them two was destined to be together. I told him I was really happy for them both. At least some good's come out of all this pain, eh?

Got another bit of good news today. Phil's okayed it for Ricky to work flexi-time, so he can stay here with us in Balham and commute to work. It'll mean long days for him, but he says he don't mind, so long as he's with me and Liam. I'm dead chuffed. I've really missed him. It was a novelty being apart to start with, but to be honest, it began to drag after a while.

It's made me realize all the little things Ricky does that I know I take for granted, like letting me have a lie-in if we've had a rough night with Liam, or telling me I look lovely when I know I look pig-ugly or bringing me a cup of tea at three o'clock in the morning when Liam wants a feed. Ricky may not set the world on fire, but that's not what you need when you've got a family. He's a great dad and he's solid and reliable and caring. And he gives great cuddles. That's what you need, not passion. Who needs all that pounding-heart stuff, anyway? I'm not sure it even exists, out in the real world. And even if it does, I'm too knackered to do anything about it. These days I'm happy if I get a good night's kip!

17 April

Our wedding anniversary. Two year's of marriage. Seems much longer! Carol and Alan baby-sat so that we could go out and me and Ricky went to a little Italian restaurant. The food was nice but we were both really tired so we went straight home afterwards. We had been meaning to go on to a club, it seems an age since we went dancing, but we were both worried about leaving Liam for too long. Silly, ain't it? I mean, I know he's in good hands. It's just that your priorities change, once you've got a kid. We spent the whole time talking about Liam, all the new things he's doing, and we just wanted to get back and be with him. I guess our wild days are over. Maybe I am becoming boring and middle-aged. I've always wanted stability and now, for the first time in my life, I've got it. Guess I shouldn't look a gift horse in the mouth, as me granddad would say. I've got more than my mum ever had, that's for sure.

20 April

Natasha would have been one year old today. We didn't talk about it much. Ricky gave me a little posy of wild flowers – daisies, buttercups, cow parsley, forget-me-knots – when he got back from work. He said he'd picked them from the grass under the trees in the cemetery and put another bunch on Natasha's grave. I was so choked, I couldn't say anything, just hugged him really tight.

26 April

Mum seems happier these days. I tried to get her to talk about things last night, when Alan was out at his stress therapy group. She said they're getting on a bit better now. We ended up drinking a bottle of cheap red wine and reminiscing about the past. I asked her who, out of all her boyfriends, she'd ever really loved, and she said David would always be the one she had something special with, but she knew she could never rely on him because he's weak.

I know what she means. He let so many people down. When he left Walford he swore he'd always be there for me, but he's never shown his face again. And as for Joe, he abandoned him because Joe was sick and he couldn't cope. I saw Joe in the mental hospital after he was diagnosed with schizophrenia.

I was really shocked at the state of him. Me and Joe still keep in touch (that was another revelation, finding out I had a half-brother) and he's OK now, but no thanks to David.

It's amazing, the webs of lies people weave because they can't face up to their actions. I mean, David was even stringing Cindy along. She was so desperate to be with him, she shot her husband. I know the market traders all reckon they wouldn't need much of an excuse to put a bullet in Ian Beale, but all the same ... you fantasize about getting revenge like that, but not many people actually do it. I got David to cough up a wardrobe of new clothes and a car cos I knew he felt guilty about not being a father to me, but it's not in the same league, is it? Just as well, or I'd have no family left...

28 April

Found out today that Louise has left the Square. Not before time. I can't think why she hung around anyway, after Simon left. She certainly won't be missed. Apparently Grant had a go at her in front of everybody and she turned round and blasted the whole pub, saying they weren't no better than her. I wish I'd been there, I'd have put her straight and no mistake. Good riddance to bad rubbish.

8 May

Ricky's finding it a real slog, commuting to Walford every day. Phil's being good about the hours, but Ricky still has to get the work done. By the time he gets home, he's good for nothing, Liam's asleep and I'm crashed out in front of the telly, ready for bed meself. Dunno whether he can keep this up much longer. Me neither, I'm worried about the stall, apart from anything else. I've got Sylvia, the temp, ringing me with daily reports, but there's nothing like keeping your hands on, is there?

Alan's much better now and him and Mum seem to have settled down into their old routine, so I don't think we'll be needed here much longer. Alan's starting a new job on Monday, portering up at the hospital! I said, what is it with you, can't you get away from the place? Anyway, he seems happy, and that's the main thing. I'd be looking forward to going home, if we had a home to go to. We're gonna have one last go at finding somewhere this weekend.

12 May

I've never seen so many dives in me life. Everything we can afford is either riddled with damp or rat-infested or on some grotty high-rise estate where the kids do drugs on the stairways. I cannot believe the property prices for renting. It's all the new offices in Docklands that's done it. All them yuppies wanting converted warehouses to live in. An estate agent told us it's had a knock-on effect everywhere round here and all the landlords have hiked their rents up. We can't even afford a tiny little terrace.

Guess I can't put it off any longer. There doesn't seem to be any choice. We're gonna have to bite the bullet and move into the Vic.

17 May

We're back in Walford. I won't say 'home', cos I ain't home. I'm in the Vic and I hate it. Got here this morning, early, so that Ricky could go to work. I could feel this knot tightening in my stomach, the nearer we got to the place. By the time we got here, I was feeling sick as a pig. I was dreading being in Tiff's room again and, when I went up there, it was even worse than I thought it would be.

They've still got the same bed, same curtains, same pictures on the wall, even the same duvet cover. I opened all the drawers and found an earring of hers down the back of one of them. It really got to me. I said to Ricky, 'We can't stay here. I can't face waking up here every morning.' I was all set to go back to

Mum's there and then. He tried to persuade me that Tiffany would want us there, but that just made me feel worse, imagining Tiff looking down on us. It's all very well Ricky saying we've got to let go of the past, but when it's shoved in your face, how can you?

I ain't just talking about Tiffany, neither. When I looked out the window, I got another shock. I saw Natalie. At first, I thought I must have imagined her, cos when I looked again, she'd disappeared. Then, when I went down to the bar later, I saw her talking to Ricky. She was all tarted up in a business suit and she'd changed her hair, but it was definitely her. She had her hand on his arm and she was leaning towards him with a big smile on her face.

It was like being thumped in the guts, seeing the two of them together. Last time I saw that scheming little cow was when I found her all over Ricky in the Arches. Natalie was the reason me and Ricky split up. She was supposed to be my friend and all the time she was being nice to my face, she was doing it with my boyfriend behind my back. She even set him up so I would find out – only planted her bra in his overalls pocket! She thought I'd dump him and she would have Ricky all to herself, but even Ricky didn't wanna know. Not that I had any sympathy for him.

I moved back home and wouldn't see Ricky or speak to him. I went on this wild revenge jag, dumping chips and vinegar all over him in Beale's Plaice, cutting up his clothes, flirting with other men right in front of him. It took us months to get over the trouble that bitch caused.

I just couldn't believe she'd had the nerve to set foot here again, after the send-off I gave her. I went round her house and slapped her and called her every name I could think of, and then some. I told her everyone wanted her out of Walford. Mum had a go at her, too, and Robbie even sprayed 'slag' on her door. She left the same day and I ain't seen her since.

37

There's only one reason Natalie would come back, and that's to finish what she started. Seeing her again made me feel so churned up, I just had to get out, so I went for a walk down by the canal. It's lucky I didn't bump into her, or I'd've pushed her straight in. Peggy saw I was upset about something, so I was forced to tell her cos she was giving me the third degree. She said I should talk to Ricky and I said, 'I don't know if he'll tell me the truth'. I mean, he lied to me last time. She said, 'Well, then you've only got one option, haven't you?'

I tracked Natalie down to the video shop, only it ain't just a video shop any more, it's where she runs this dating agency. 'Romantic Relations', that was the sign on the door. Handy for a slapper. She can't have thought hard to come up with that one. I walked straight in and told her she wasn't welcome here. We had a right ding-dong and she said she wasn't after Ricky, she was with Barry. She was going on about how Ricky had helped her sort things out with Barry while I was away, which really made me see red. I was right in her face, poking her and shouting, 'I don't care why you've come back, I want you out of here and I ain't gonna stop bothering you until you go.' Only this time, she didn't run away. She didn't even scream back at me. She just said she'd moved on and it was about time I did, too. What's her game?

18 May

I know I've been a right cow to everybody today, but I just can't help it. I was so wound up about Ricky and Natalie, I couldn't sleep a wink last night, even though Frank and Peggy let us have their room cos of how I felt about sleeping in Tiff's bed. I just lay there thinking, Natalie's been back here for ages and Ricky ain't only known about it, he's been pally with her. Why ain't he told me? Cos he's got something to hide, that's why. And why ain't anyone else said nothing? Robbie's been here all this time, and Pat. They both know what happened before. How come neither of them told me? Cos they're covering for him, that's why. And it went on and on, round and round my head, 'til I got up this morning, by which time I was in a stinking mood with the world and his wife.

It was like, today was crunch time. I mean, there's no point putting the thumbscrews on. Ricky knows how I feel about Natalie. And he knows that I'm gonna run in to her, sooner or later. I thought, if he don't say anything, that's it, I'll know for sure something's been going on. Just as well he came and confessed when he did. I was ready to commit murder by coffee time.

He came back to the Vic looking all sheepish and said there was something he needed to tell me. Then he said, 'You remember Natalie?' – like I'm gonna forget her, as if. I just stared at him and he mumbled, 'Seems she's back in Walford. Sort of permanent.'

I went, 'I see. And how long have you known she was back?' and he got all flustered and said just this morning, but he hadn't actually spoken to her. I screamed at him, 'You liar!' and told him he was a complete pig. I said, 'If I find out anything's goin' on between you and that tart, we're finished, d'you hear me?'

I could just see it all happening again, and, when I get scared, I go on the attack. I was horrible to Pat, too, but she gave it back, saying Ricky worshipped the ground I walked on and I should start appreciating what I'd got. It gave me something to think about, and when Ricky came back into the Vic later, I apologized. I told him, it's just that so much has happened these past few months and everything's changed and I feel like I can't rely on anything any more. It's as if everything's slipping through my fingers and my life's spinning out of control. The reason I get so ratty with Ricky is cos, deep down, I'm afraid of losing him, too.

24 May

I can't cope with this. I feel as if I'm being stifled. We're all under each other's feet at the Vic and Peggy's taken charge of Liam, telling me I can't pick him up because she's just got him off, like he's her son instead of mine. She's made her own little routine for him already. If we're there for much longer, he'll turn out like Grant. I mean, I hardly see him all day, cos I'm back on the stall, and when I do get home all I want to do is cuddle him but he's usually out for the count by then.

On top of that, I've had Natalie in my face every time I turn round. She tried being nice to me this morning, but I told her to drop dead. If she thinks I'll so much as pass the time of day with her, she's mistaken. She seems to spend all her time with Barry draped round her, like he's some sort of fashion accessory – which he probably is, in her case. I warned him. I said, 'Natalie's playing you for a mug 'til she makes her move on Ricky', but he had a right go at me and said I was off my head.

By the end of the day I didn't want to go anywhere near the Vic, so I arranged to meet up with Ricky in the caff. It's come to something when the caff's the only place we can be together. We certainly ain't got no privacy at home. Ricky says we've got to look on the bright side – we aren't paying rent so we can save up for a deposit on somewhere to buy, perhaps with a garden for Liam. I suppose he's got a point, but if he thinks I'm letting Peggy walk all over me he's got another think coming. If it gets too much, we're moving out and that's an end to it.

27 May

I thought I knew what I wanted out of my life, but since I've had Liam I ain't sure about anything any more. Take the stall. Ever since I first started out selling, it's been my life. Up until then, I'd only had crap jobs, working in the chippy or the caff or the video shop – not that any of them lasted more than five minutes. Then Sanjay and Gita gave me a chance to help out on their stall, and I was hooked, straight off. I've always been interested in fashion, and everything just seemed to slot into place. It was like finding a missing piece of jigsaw. Next thing I was going on buying trips and ordering new stock, then I organized a fashion show and sold loads of gear and it was brilliant – a real rush.

For the first time in my life I was a success at something. I got me own stall, persuaded Ricky to invest in it, chatted up the bank manager and suddenly I was a career woman. It all seemed to happen so fast. One minute I was shovelling chips, and the next I was talking business plans. Since then, I've thrown everything into that stall. And now I feel like throwing it all away.

It's Liam. I just miss him so much. I though it might be easier this time, now he's a little bit older, but it ain't. If anything, it's harder. Ricky can't see that. He didn't like me helping Tony out before, but now he's all for me working so that we can get some savings behind us. I want that, too – it's just that I'm not sure I've got what it takes any more. Everyone else is looking after my baby except me. Sonia's feeding him, Pat's taking him out for walks, Peggy's bathing him and putting him to bed. It's like I've become this wage slave – and for what? My son's the most important thing in my life, and if I can't be with him, there's no point in working, is there?

31 May

I didn't think my life could get much worse, but it just has. Mum turned up on the doorstep this evening, complete with luggage. She's left Alan. After everything I did to being them back together! I really thought they were gonna be OK. I can't believe it. The family's falling apart. Peggy said Mum could sleep on the sofa, so that's where she is.

We're like a bunch of refugees, all camped out at the Vic. When I think we had a father, a home, all of us kids were together, and now look at us. I just feel so angry with Mum. Why is she doing this to us again?

Even before Mum put in her surprise appearance, I already had the Bank Holiday from hell. Frank decided to take precious Peggy on a little outing – with Liam – leaving me and Ricky to run the bar. It was all cooked up before I was even out of bed. When I came in to breakfast I saw Ricky looking guilty and I knew something was up. We were supposed to be having a family day out ourselves. I said to Frank, 'So that's why you wanted us living here – a couple of mugs to hold the fort whenever you decide to swan off!' I told Frank no way, but then Ricky said he'd already agreed. Honestly, he's a waste of space sometimes, and I didn't hold back from letting him know it.

I wasn't gonna help behind the bar, but Ricky told me I was selfish and ungrateful and in the end I gave in just to get some peace. The bar was heaving and we were rushed off our feet, especially as Nina had to get off to a tutorial. I could just about stick it – although seeing Barry and Natalie eating each other's faces made me want to vomit – until the little tart waltzed over and said she wanted to thank Ricky for helping them to find somewhere to live.

I dragged him out back and asked what she meant, and he said he'd mentioned to Barry and Natalie that they'd finished doing the old squat up. I said, 'I don't suppose you thought it would have been perfect for us, did you?' and he went 'it just sort of slipped out'. I thought I was gonna explode. I just grabbed me coat and left him to deal with the punters. It was that or kill him.

By the time I got back, the bar was in total chaos, Peggy and Frank were back, Liam was overtired and screaming and Mum was upstairs with her suitcases. Perfect end to a perfect day.

1 June

Mum's got a bloke. I knew it. She's always got another one lined up, ready and waiting. She never just ups and leaves. Not that she admitted it to us straight off. I had to get it out of her. I said, 'There's someone else, isn't there?' She tried to wriggle off the hook, going, 'We've been over this', but she knew I wasn't gonna let it drop. She said, 'Don't look at me like that. It was already over when I met Dan.' I thought, oh, great, here we go again. She said I'd like him and I said, 'No I wouldn't, and don't tell me nothing about him, either', and I stormed out.

I don't get Mum, sometimes. I mean, she's behaving like an irresponsible teenager, flitting from bloke to bloke ... and she's left Billy behind. I don't know how she can do that, abandon her own son. She said he hadn't been deserted, he was settled in at school and it made sense in the short term for him to stay with Alan. I still don't understand how she can put herself before her child, though. Now I've got Liam, I could never do that.

I went back to see her later when I'd calmed down a bit ... as Ricky pointed out, she did come to me, not this 'Dan', which is something. She said things were definitely finished with Alan and they'd only staggered on as long as they did because they thought they ought to give it one more try for our sakes. I felt guilty then, but she said it was no-one's fault. There was just too much water under the bridge. I asked where Dan fitted in to all this, and she said they met a while ago but he'd just been a shoulder to cry on and it was only in the last few weeks she'd realized there was something more going on.

I went, 'Not like you to be so slow', which was a bit bitchy, but I was really hurting. I can't bear the thought of not seeing Billy, or Alan. And Sonia's beside herself ... I found her in the Square in floods of tears. It's all very well Mum following her heart, but where does that leave the rest of us?

Had a fight with Natalie today. She's been getting right up my nose, swanning round the Square with Barry like they're joined at the hip. She was in the Vic this evening, all over him as usual. I said, 'For God's sake, Barry, we don't all want to see your tongue in her ear,' and she went, 'Don't listen to her, she's just jealous'. I said, 'Oh yeah, and what have you got that I want?', and she said, 'For a start, somewhere to live and someone I want to live with, it's called a life but you've probably forgotten about all that.'

I was so riled, I said, 'At least I don't go leaping into bed with my best mate's boyfriend,' and then she had the nerve to go, 'And she was the one who was having it off with married men while she was still in the fifth year.' So I slapped her. Right across the face. She had it coming. She grabbed my hair and started yanking it and the next thing we were scrapping like a couple of schoolgirls. It's just a shame Peggy stopped us before I could do her any real damage. At least she threw Natalie out, though I got a rollicking too.

I don't know what's happening to me. I just seem to be losing it. I feel as wound up as a coiled spring. Anything happens and … bam … off I go. Ricky's been driving me mental, too. Everything he does annoys me. It's like he sets out to do it. I mean, he knows what'll start me off and he just seems to do it all the time. I don't even like him touching me at the moment.

He's making all these assumptions about what we're gonna do, settle down in Walford, get a house, have another baby … without even consulting me. I told him, who said we've got to stay in this dump? The trouble with Ricky is, he's got no ambition. He'd be happy to work at the Arches for the rest of his days. I want something more than that. I don't know what. I just know that I ain't happy with what I've got.

Maybe it's Mum. Thinking about her situation has made me see the similarities between us. I mean, Mum and Alan had the most solid relationship on the planet, and if they can't make it work, what hope is there for the rest of us? It just goes to show, marriage is all a con. Nothing lasts for ever. Mum and Alan were all right until he sprang that surprise wedding on her. It was dead romantic at the time, but she said after that they stopped working at things and took each other for granted.

Sounds familiar. There's supposed to be two of us in this marriage, and where is Ricky right now? He said he'd baby-sit Liam tonight so I could go out for a drink with Mum. I bet he's forgotten all about it. I'm sitting here, twiddling me thumbs, and as usual he's carrying on in his own sweet way.

8 June

God, what a night. I feel bad about what I wrote yesterday, but how was I supposed to know Ricky was in casualty? I was getting more and more angry cos he missed Liam's bedtime, and I was just about to go out and look for him when I got a call from the hospital saying he'd been admitted with a head injury. I went flying down there and who should I find waiting in Reception, but Natalie!

Ricky was strapped to a board and had this collar round his neck. He was groaning and mumbling and he didn't seem to recognize me. Natalie said they were doing tests but it was too early to say what was wrong with him. My first thought was she'd hurt Ricky to get back at me. I said, 'What have you done to him?', and she said she hadn't done nothing, he'd hit his head in the Arches. When I asked what the hell she was doing round there, she said she'd gone to tell Ricky to sort me out. We ended up having a barney in the cubicle and a nurse came in and said, 'This is a casualty department, not the Jerry Springer Show', and chucked us out. I went and sat in the relatives' room and Natalie followed me in there an' all. I told her to sling her hook but she started raking up the past, all this stuff about how me and Tiff used to gang up on her at school and she always got left out of things. We had another scream-ing match and got thrown out of there as well.

Then I found out they'd taken Ricky for a CT scan, and it really hit home how serious it might be. Tiff had a CT scan after she fell down the stairs. It showed she had a blood clot on the brain. She was unconscious for days. I remember sitting by her bedside, watching her lying there, not moving. No-one knew whether she'd come out of her coma and, if she did, whether she'd have brain damage or not. I thought I'd lost her. I couldn't go through that again.

Natalie found me in tears in reception and I ended up telling her about what happened to Tiff. Even though we was all at school together, Natalie didn't really know Tiff, not like I did. She said she always thought Tiff was 'a bit rough'. I told her, Tiff was lovely, a bit wild, but then we all were. Then she became Mrs Mitchell and grew up quick, but she was always the same with me. If I'm honest, I cared about her more than Ricky. We had this bond, we could row, but we'd always make up, we were always really good friends. I miss her so much, it's like a physical ache in my chest sometimes.

I couldn't bear waiting in casualty any longer ... it was all too much, being in that place again. It wasn't just Tiff I lost there, it was Natasha, too. I went outside and sat on a bench in the dark, watching the night buses go past and the drunks stumbling out of the pub opposite. It was good just to be back in the real world, breathe fresh air, see life going on as normal. Inside the hospital, it's like a different existence. And what goes on in there can change the rest of your life. For ever.

Nat came out too and brought me a cup of tea. I told her all about Natasha. It was easier to talk in the dark. I told her how beautiful my little baby was. We both ended up weeping. It brought us together, somehow. Once we started talking prop-erly, 'stead of just shouting at each other, I remembered what good mates we used to be.

It was such a relief to have Nat with me when the doctor came to tell me about Ricky. I was convinced Ricky was gonna die and when she said 'Mrs Butcher', in that way doctors have, like they're about to give you bad news, my heart was in my mouth. Then she said, 'Your husband's a lot brighter', and I could have kissed her. She said Ricky had a bit of bruising on the brain but nothing serious and he just had to stay in for a couple of days so they could keep an eye on him. I said, 'He's really gonna be all right?', cos I could hardly believe it, and she said yes, thanks to his thick skull he was just gonna have a bad headache. Suppose next time I tell Ricky to get something through his thick head, I've gotta be grateful that it is!

Me and Nat shared a cab back to the Vic and I asked her in for a night-cap. Peggy came down in her dressing gown and found us and I thought she was gonna hit the roof, cos she'd barred Nat, but she was OK when she saw we was friends. It's like all the poison's drained out of me, now. I know Nat ain't after Ricky... she said it was the real thing with her and Barry. Takes all sorts, dunnit? I warned her, marriage ain't all it's cracked up to be. Still, whatever makes her happy. The main thing is, I've got Nat back on side again. I think we'll be all right from now on.

10 June

Ricky's home, a bit woozy but otherwise fine. He's gone back to work today. I've told him not to go under any car bonnets for a while, I couldn't handle any more shocks.

Grant's been really off with me, I mean, more off than usual; he was vicious when I made some comment about Courtney this morning, then later on I found out the reason, cos Peggy had a go, too. They think I shopped him to the social services. This social worker came round the other day saying they'd had a report about Courtney and Grant threw him out the house. Then he smashed the bloke's car window and a copper arrested him. (It was the night Ricky got taken into hospital, cos me and Nat spotted Grant up the scaffolding by the bridge when we got home, and he tried to pour whisky on my head. Now I know why.)

I was furious with Peggy for even thinking I'd do such a thing. Whatever my opinion is of Grant, I wouldn't want to see Courtney taken into care. What kind of a friend to Tiff would that make me? I can find fault with Grant about most things, but not about how he treats Courtney. Like I said to Frank, Grant's always been a good dad. Rotten husband, lousy bloke, but good dad. Frank said he'd sort it out and not to worry, but I don't like being treated like a grass.

14 June

Mum and Sonia have moved in with Robbie, Matthew, Lenny and Lisa ... Robbie's on the sofa and they've got his room. Can't say I envy them, knowing Robbie's personal hygiene, but Peggy's been dropping hints about the Vic being overcrowded so Mum had to find somewhere else to live and she insisted on taking Sonia with her. Sonia's in a right sulk about it, but then she ain't had a good word to say to Mum since she arrived. Of all of us, she's probably the closest to Alan, and she's taken them splitting up really hard. I ain't happy about it either, I mean, I always thought Mum and Alan were perfect together, but it's the thought of this new bloke that bothers me the most. I know he'll mess her around and she'll end up getting hurt. It'll be the same old story. And we'll have to pick up the pieces.

Frank bent my ear about it today, cos he could see I was being a bit frosty with Mum. Then he said Phil and Grant were just the same with him and Peggy at first, but they came round because they realized he was good for her. It gave me something to think about, cos I knew Frank understood where I was coming from. In the end I went and gave Mum a hand moving her stuff into Robbie's and afterwards we went for a drink and watched Terry singing (he wasn't bad, though I say it myself). I suppose I was calling a truce. I even asked about Dan. Mum said he was gorgeous and very romantic and he really loved her. Not bad for starters, but I ain't rolling over and saying he's Mr Wonderful yet.

17 June

Ricky's met Dan. So has Robbie. They both seem to have joined his fan club. He came to the caff this morning and brought Mum flowers. Sounds like a smarmy creep to me. I was hacked off with Ricky for not telling me Dan was over there, cos I wanted to suss him out for myself, but he said he did mention it and Mum didn't think it was the right time ... thought I'd be nasty to her new boyfriend, I expect. I could've gone over and checked him out – Ricky said he thought Dan was still over there – but if Mum can't be bothered to introduce him to me, I ain't gonna make a special effort. All I can say is, if he ain't man enough to cope with a frank opinion from me, then he can't be up to much, can he?

21 June

For ages now I've been feelin' kind of empty and flat, like there's something missing from my life, and today I think I found out what it is. I don't feel I've really achieved anything. I'm a wife and mother and that's it. OK, I've got the stall, but freezing my bum off on in a street market all day don't exactly make me businesswoman of the year.

Ricky's been on about having another baby – he brought it up again this morning – but I can't even think about that right now. I just want to do something different. If we have another kid, I can kiss any chance of that goodbye for another eighteen years. By the time I've brought up Ricky's brood I'll be past doing anything.

Trouble is, I just haven't known what it was I wanted to do. Then, this morning, I got talking to Sarah Hills in the caff. She's studying to go to uni and she was telling me how much it's changed these days. It's not all airy-fairy courses, they've got these practical courses, vocational they call them. She showed me the prospectus and it looked really good. Apparently, they like 'mature students' for that sort of thing. They've got this wicked course in fashion at Brighton. I got the bit between my teeth and rang up for an application form.

Ricky wasn't very happy when I told him, but then he thinks the world starts and ends in Walford. I told him, Brighton's a happening place, loads of young people and clubs and all that, but he went into a grouch for the rest of the evening. He's so unsupportive, sometimes.

The other bit of news is that Mum's trying to persuade us all to come to Southend with her and Dan this weekend, to meet him properly. She said he's got this flat belonging to a mate and we could all have a bit of a holiday, spend some time together. Sonia threw a complete wobbly and stormed out, saying we'd all be being unfaithful to Alan. She's got a point, but Mum looked really upset. Even I felt sorry for her.

22 June

Walford's headline news today. That Saskia girl's been found murdered – her body's been dug up in Epping Forest. I know I shouldn't say this, but I always thought she was a right stuck-up little cow. She was a bit weird, too, couldn't put my finger on what it was about her, but she was definitely a bit wacko.

Anyway, on a brighter note, I've decided to go to Southend with the others. I talked Ricky into it – we're gonna go on Friday, spend a night in Brighton first, give me a chance to look at the college. I know it's early days and I've not even applied yet, but I want to get a feel for the place. I'm really excited. I've got good vibes about this. I ain't so chuffed about seeing this

Dan – it just feels way too rushed, somehow – but I feel I ought to do it for Mum's sake. Sonia's still refusing to budge but it ain't fair not to give the guy a chance. How bad can it be?

25 June

Brighton's pretty cool. Just how I thought it would be. I feel right, here. I think living in Walford is beginning to make me old before my time. Let's face it, Albert Square ain't exactly a Mecca for fashion and a night out at the Vic ain't what I'd call hitting the high spots. It's such a narrow little world ... all the backbiting, gossiping, arguing. You'd think life ended down the bottom of George Street, the way some people carry on. I said to Ricky, I don't want Liam growing up like that.

Down here it's like there's room to breathe, shake off some of the ghosts, start afresh. I can be young again. I'm not even twenty-two yet, for heaven's sakes! I've seen loads of people our age with kids walking along the seafront and drinking outside pubs and they're all trendy looking and modern. I'm sure we'd fit right in. And we could have another baby after I've finished college, so Ricky would be happy and Liam would have a brother or sister. Ricky seemed to be OK with that. I know he really wants a baby now, but a few years don't make much difference. I think I've talked him round. It's really nice to spend some time by ourselves, just strolling along eating ice-creams and watching the world go by. I feel as if a weight's lifting off my shoulders. We've booked into a B & B for tonight. I'm quite looking forward to it. What do they say? A change is as good as a rest? It's not often we get the chance for a dirty weekend, after all!

26 June

It's 3 a.m., and I'm writing this by the light of the street lamp shining through the cracks in the bedroom curtains. I had to get this down straight away. I'm so desperate to tell somebody and there's no-one I can turn to here. We're in Southend, with Mum, Robbie, Sonia (I persuaded her to come at the last moment) ... and Dan. The mystery man. Only, he ain't. Talk about the past coming back to haunt you.

I already know him. Too well, as it happens. We slept together when I was fifteen. We only did it four or five times – he was the one that dumped me when he found out my age, but he broke my heart all the same. I got the shock of my life when I saw him again. I came out of the bedroom and Mum went, 'Bianca, this is Dan'. She was standing beside him, smiling nervously. Me and Dan just stared at each other. It was like in a film, when time stops. I didn't know what to say ... for once. It's not often I'm lost for words, but I really, truly had no idea what to do. My mind just seemed to have seized up. I was like a rabbit, caught in the headlights, unable to move. I dunno how long we stood like that – long enough, cos I heard Mum clear her throat, and I thought, she's realized, she can see it written all over our faces.

Then Dan stepped forward and said, 'Bianca, it's nice to meet you, at last', and I knew then how he was gonna play it. I muttered something like, 'Yeah, and you'. After that, everybody went back to what they'd been doing and time carried on again, like nothing had happened, except that me and Dan were still staring at each other. Mum started asking who wanted pizza for dinner, and Sonia and Robbie were arguing about the telly and Ricky was bouncing Liam on his lap. I just had to get away and I fled back into the bedroom. My heart was thumping really fast and my mouth was all dry. I had to sit down on the bed cos my legs were so weak and wobbly.

I must have looked rough because when Mum came in to see what I made of Dan, she thought I was ill. I didn't say anything about him and me – how could I? – I just said I was tired. She told me to have a lie down until dinner, but I knew I'd have to face him then and I didn't know if I could handle it. All this stuff was racing round my head, like, did he know about me? Had he tracked me down through Mum? It was too mad to be a coincidence, him turning up like this.

He got me on my own later, when I went out to the kitchen to fetch the plates. I said, 'What the hell's going on?' and he said, 'Bea – that was short for Bianca, was it?' cos that's what I told him my name was originally. He said he had no idea me and Mum was related, until today, which I found hard to believe. I said, 'This is some kind of sick joke, ain't it?' and he went, 'I wish it was'. We didn't have the chance to say any more, cos Ricky came in to get the beers, and after that there just wasn't an opportunity. Somehow I managed to hold it together but I couldn't eat anything, and being in the same room with Dan was a total nightmare. Luckily, Sonia was being a real cow, which distracted them all a bit. I spent most of the evening with Liam, pretending he wouldn't settle, then turned in early.

Of course, I couldn't sleep a wink. I was tossing and turning, wondering what to do, while Ricky snored away beside me, out for the count. All I could think of was how much Dan had hurt me, chucking me the way he did, and I knew he'd do the same thing to Mum. He was a womanizer when I knew him, six years ago. I knew he was married, but I didn't care then. You don't think about other people's relationships when you're that age. I was just out for a good time and Dan was older, handsome, flash with his cash, and very experienced. He wasn't my first, but he did things in bed – well, let's just say that after the boys I'd slept with, Dan was a revelation. He was also a drinker. He used to drink himself almost unconscious some nights. You don't get an alcoholic adulterer with a taste for young girls suddenly turning into a saint.

About midnight, the door creaked opened a bit and I saw Dan looking in. He didn't say nothing, just disappeared, but I got the message. I found him in the kitchen, sitting in the dark, waiting for me. He said, 'I thought we needed to talk', and I said, 'Well, I'll make this quick, shall I? Tomorrow morning you pack your things, make up some excuse to my mum and then you get the hell out of our lives.'

It's the only solution that makes sense and I thought he'd see that, but he said he wasn't gonna. He said that Mum really loved him and for the first time in his life he had something really special with someone. That hurt, especially when he said that all I'd been to him was a dirty little slut. I told him he wasn't good enough for Mum, but he said he was different now, he'd changed.

I said, 'That doesn't change what happened. You can't carry on seeing her now', but Dan don't see it that way. He's happy to just ignore our past. Then he said, 'How do you think Ricky would take the news?' and he dared me to wake him up and tell him everything. I knew I couldn't. I've never mentioned Dan to Ricky ... don't know why, didn't want to shock him I suppose. Ricky's such an innocent, in many ways. I mean, I know he's cheated on me once, but this business with Dan – well, it's out of his league. If I sprung it on Ricky now, he'd be dead suspicious, blow it up out of all proportion. He'd feel betrayed, which is silly cos it was way before him and me got together. I suppose I should've said summat – I'm the one that's always banging on about us being honest with each other – but it's just not relevant, so why stir things up? It'll only cause trouble between us. I'll just have to be extra careful to keep this diary hidden from now on. Ricky knows I keep it, but I've made him swear never to read it. It's one of them ones with a lock on it. All the same, I ain't gonna leave it lying around any more. I wouldn't want him to find out about Dan that way. Anyway, I need somewhere to spill my secrets...

As for Mum ... if she knew her wonderful new boyfriend had been screwing her fifteen-year-old daughter, she would ditch him as soon as look at him. I told Dan that and he said if

I was so sure Mum had to know, I'd have to be the one to tell her. We was still arguing when a light went on in the living room and Mum walked in. Dan made some excuse about hearing a noise and finding me in the kitchen making tea and Mum believed him. She said, 'You two have been talking about me, haven't you?' and for a horrible moment I thought she'd been listening at the door. Then Dan said, yeah, I'd been giving him the third degree, and Mum went to me, 'So what do you think? Does he pass?'

What could I say? She looked so happy and hopeful. I knew I couldn't tell her right then. I'll have to find the right time. I said, 'Yeah, for now', and she looked pleased and dragged Dan off to bed.

I can see the dawn breaking now, pink streaks of light in the inky blue sky. There are seagulls calling outside. A milk lorry has just gone past in the street below. A new day gearing up. I don't know how I'm gonna face it.

27 June

I made sure Mum and me got some time together today by suggesting Ricky and Dan went for a pint while we did some girly shopping. Mum was quite taken with the idea but I could see Dan was worried. I thought, good, that'll keep him on his toes, show him I mean business. I wasn't sure exactly what I was gonna say to Mum, but I had to sound her out.

Once we were alone, I think Mum was expecting me to mouth off about Dan – she said she'd never known me keep quiet for so long about something – but I said I just wanted to know how well she knew him. She said she knew he'd been divorced, blamed himself and had a son that he didn't see, and that was as much as she wanted to know at this stage. I told her Dan didn't seem her type, but she said he was exactly her type and he encouraged her to put herself first and that was what she needed right now, to do the things she'd missed out on. I said, 'By having me, you mean', and she admitted it. She said she'd missed out on her twenties bringing me and Robbie up and that Dan had brought her back to life.

All the while I was despairing inside, cos I could see Mum was really happy and I knew I was gonna destroy that if I said anything. She gave me the chance, she asked me what it was I didn't like about Dan, but once again I couldn't do it. I just shook my head, like a little girl. Mum thought I was being self-ish. She said she thought I of all people would be the one to understand how she felt. I thought, if only you knew, Mum, if only you knew.

I knew Dan was rattled, cos he and Ricky came to meet us and the first thing Dan said was, 'Everything all right?' I saw a glimmer of hope then, and thought, if he's that worried and I keep the pressure up on him, I can get him to do the job for me by breaking it off with Mum. That was my plan. But when we got back to the flat, Dan followed me into the bedroom and backed me up against the wall. He was right in my face, towering over me, and he was really angry. He said I wasn't gonna spoil his happiness over nothing and that all we ever had was cheap, meaningless and best forgotten. It was like a slap in the face.

I wasn't scared – well, not exactly – but being up so close to him really shook me. Everything about his face was so familiar. I got this sudden flashback of the last time we were that close. He was making love to me and staring down into my eyes with that same intense expression. I felt disgusted with myself for thinking that, especially after what he'd just said about us. That was what left me shaking, not his bullying threats.

Then, just as we was all about to leave, Dan really called my bluff. Mum got us all together and said they had something to tell us. My heart went into my mouth, cos I thought maybe he'd told her after all, then she said she and Dan had decided to live together. I was totally stunned. I said, 'When was this all decided?' and Dan said a few minutes ago. Then he had the nerve to lean over and kiss me on the cheek! He whispered, 'Just do everyone a favour and smile', and then he put on this big public display, going, 'There, that wasn't too tough, was it?' It was sick-making. I wanted to punch his lights out, but I had to smile, for Mum's sake. He's a total creep. I can't think what I ever saw in him. I know one thing, though. He'll trip up sooner or later. And I'll be there cheering when he does.

28 June

Everything's eating away at me. I feel so trapped. Dan's got everyone fooled. He's even starting to win Sonia round. And now he's moving in with Mum and they're going to play happy families in our old house, number 25 Albert Square (it came back on the market for rent and Mum snapped it up last week). Mum even asked if me and Ricky and Liam wanted to move in as well, cos she knows how I feel about the Vic. Stuck, aren't I? Living at the Vic's a nightmare, especially now that Ricky's snotty little sister Janine has come to stay. She's driving me up the wall already with her attitude, and she's really inconsiderate about Liam. I'm having enough trouble getting him to sleep as it is, without having her music turned up full volume. But when the alternative's moving in with my ex-lover, what choice have I got? I told Mum I couldn't turn the clock back and be one of her brood again, but that ain't the real reason. I think she's sussed.

Met Natalie for a quick coffee at Giuseppe's this afternoon and filled her in on my weekend from hell. Turns out she saw Dan on Friday and recognized him, but we'd already left for Brighton when she came to warn me. Nat thinks Mum and Ricky deserve to know the truth. I said, 'What am I supposed to say? "Funny old life, isn't it, Mum, your last lover being one of my first? Oh, and by the way, he's a slime-ball".' I mean, no-one deserves that, do they?

Natalie knows all about Dan, cos I introduced them at a party once, and she remembers what a mess I was when he ditched me, crying me eyes out at school. I said, 'I had a crush on him, of course I cried. I was too stupid to know a creep when I saw one.' She went, 'Good-looking creep though.' I mean, excuse me? This is from a woman who thinks Barry Evans is gorgeous. Me and Nat may be friends again, but that don't mean I think she's got taste in men. Anyway, I told her, Dan's gone podgy now. Whatever he might have had once, he's lost it as far as I'm concerned.

29 June

Had a blast at Peggy today. She and Frank both treat Janine as if she's a princess, whereas I can see straight through her. She's a lazy, conniving little cow who turns on the charm when she wants something and won't lift a finger for anyone unless it suits her. The final straw was when Peggy asked me to make Janine's tea for her! Just cos Frank's poor little hard-done-by daughter had actually done something for a change – she helped Dan and Robbie and Sonia decorate number 25 – Peggy seems to think she should be waited on hand and foot. And I've been on the stall all day, working!

I said, 'I appreciate you having your poor relations under your roof, but I'm not going to pay for it by being a servant for that spoilt brat!' Ricky had a go at me afterwards, then I had Frank chasing after me. I knew I shouldn't have said it, but I'm so tense at the moment, what with this Dan business. I thought Frank was gonna give me an earful, too, but he said he understood how I felt about living with the family and that a change of scenery might do us good. You could've knocked me over with a feather! I thought Frank of all people would want Ricky to stay in Walford. He said he's got contacts all over the place and he might be able to fix Ricky up with a job. It's something to think about.

I can't go on living like this. I can't bear being around Dan, it keeps bringing back memories. Bad memories. Caught him looking at me today, when me and Ricky went round to see new paintwork. He was arsing about, pretending to be that poncy bloke on *Changing Rooms*, and I found myself laughing, though I hadn't meant to. It gave me a flashback of how Dan used to be – funny, spontaneous, a bit OTT. He never acted his age. I know that's what Mum likes about him, but she ain't seen the other side yet. Wait 'til Dan sees someone else who takes his fancy. Then she'll find out just how impulsive he can be.

That's why I want Dan to clear off. Mum's been hurt enough times as it is. She's a survivor, cos she's had to be, but that don't mean she don't feel things, it just means she don't show how much she's suffering. Dan came into the launderette this afternoon – I think he followed me in there – and said he wanted to know if I was planning to break Mum's heart. Me break Mum's heart! That's a laugh. I mean, he's the expert. I told him I didn't need to say anything to her, cos it wouldn't be long before Mum saw his true colours. We had a row and he ended up shouting at me to grow up, like I was fifteen again. Arrogant pig. God, I hate that man.

PS. The Square's crawling with coppers. Steve Owen and Matt Rose have both been arrested for Saskia's murder. I could believe it of Steve, but Matt? He's just a kid.

1 July

Woke up feeling grotty – probably because I didn't get much sleep last night – and couldn't face going out. I just wanted to hide myself away, especially from Mum and Dan. I wasn't really ill, just a bit under the weather, but I admit I played it up a bit. The last thing I wanted to have to do was go out on the stall and smile and be nice to people. Ricky said he'd sort out some cover and he phoned Mick, cos he's looking for work. Mick said he'd do it, so that was the stall sorted, but by lunchtime I was almost beginning to wish I was out on the market than stuck in the Vic, what with one thing and another.

First of all Peggy had a dig at me – things are still a bit frosty after my outburst the other day – then that thieving little toe-rag Janine tried to go out wearing my jacket. I made her take it off, but Frank must've given her some dosh, cos not long after I sent her packing she came back upstairs swanking around in a brand new one, which she'd bought off my stall, just to rub my nose in it. I said, 'I had a different class of punter in mind when I chose that,' and she got the hump and stormed off, so at least that was one-nil to me.

Next Mum came up to see how I was and invited us over for house-warming drinks. She can read me like a book and she knew I wasn't telling her the whole story, so in the end I lied and said it was living in the Vic that was the problem. I mean, that in itself ain't a lie, cos I'm hacked off with it here, but that ain't why I've been avoiding her. Mum said all the more reason to move in with them, which wasn't what I wanted to hear.

I mean, imagine me sharing a bathroom with Dan! He and I did it in the bath, once, in this posh hotel … all bubbles and Champagne, just like in *Pretty Woman*. It would be too embarrassing, meeting on the landing. And the thought of him and Mum doing it … that's even worse. The walls are thin in that house. I think it would make me physically sick, to hear them two bonking, knowing what Dan's like. Ugh. It gives me the shivers, just thinking about it.

In the end, me and Ricky did go over to theirs for a drink, because Janine and Peggy were driving me nuts and I knew I'd explode if I stayed in the same room any longer. Dan didn't seem that pleased to see me, and we had words when the others was upstairs. I told him he had no idea how hard it was for me, seeing him with Mum. He said, 'But we're history, so what's the problem? We had a good time, didn't we?' and I went, 'Not really, no. Except in bed and that don't mean nothing.'

Putting on the glitz in my young, free and single days, back in 1995 (well, OK, it was a between-Ricky phase).

Pinched from the family album: the Jacksons, taken soon after we arrived in the Square in 1993. Billy, Mum and Sonia at the front, me, Alan and Robbie behind. Don't we all look young?

Like mother, like daughter?
Me and Mum are either the
best of friends or at each
other's throats — more like
sisters really! But then there
is only 15 years between us...

Finding out David Wicks was
my Dad was the biggest shock
of my life. To think, I used to
fancy him! Course, he didn't
tell me the truth 'til I tried to
kiss him... I was so angry, I
hit him where it hurt most —
in his wallet.

Me and Jiff had some wicked times together, especially when we went man-hunting. We'd go to a hotel bar and the blokes used to fall at our feet. Well, who could resist this fruity little number, eh?

My half-brother, Joe (David's son). More family I never knew I had!

Nat the rat, back in '94 when we was still mates. Then I found out she was sleeping with my Ricky and sent her packing with a right good slapping...

Sunny Spain, 1995, on holiday with the lads. Ricky proposed and I said yes!

On the stall. Dunno what Ricky was after, but he definitely ain't getting none!

Me, Jiff and Courtney. If only Jiff could see how her little girl's grown up now...

Ricky, sexy speedway star! He was drop-dead gorgeous in his leathers!

Wedding Day, 17 April 1997. Ricky turned up covered in mud and smelling like a farmyard, but at least I got him up the aisle in the end!

Here's Liam —
isn't he lovely? He
looks just like his
proud Daddy...

Things fall apart
between me and Ricky.
We've always been a bit
up and down but this
year it's been downhill
all the way.

I couldn't believe it when I found out who Mum's new boyfriend was — my ex, Dan!

Falling in love again … Dan and I fought against it, but neither of us was strong enough to resist.

Then Ricky cracked open some Champagne we'd brought with us and Dan made this snide toast to the future, saying he hoped it was better than the past. He was really larding it on, making a big fuss of Mum, hands all over each other like a couple of teenagers. I'm sure it was to wind me up, because of what I'd said about the sex. Then he gave her this big, full-on kiss – all tongues, you could see it! – which was really gross to watch. It was like he was throwing down a challenge.

When they went out the room to get more Champagne, I took Ricky by surprise and snogged him. It was a spur-of-the-moment thing. I don't quite know why I did it. Ricky didn't complain, of course, but he thought it was a bit strange. I said, 'We're married, aren't we? We love each other, don't we?' I mean, I shouldn't have to explain why I'm kissing my husband!

I suppose I needed to prove to myself that what me and Ricky have got after all this time together is stronger than what Mum and Dan have got after knowing each other for five minutes. The awful thing is, though, I'm not sure. When I kissed Ricky I just didn't feel anything. I remember, with Dan, my knees used to almost buckle and my stomach would flip over. I don't think I've ever had that with Ricky, not even at the start. So what does that say for our marriage?

5 July

I'm spending all my time wishing I could turn the clock back. It's doing my head in, seeing Mum and Dan together. I wish I'd just told Mum outright, at the start, when I first clapped eyes on Dan. It would've been a shock but she'd have got over it and Dan would be off the scene by now, out of our lives.

As it is, Dan ain't gonna take the hint and Mum's so wrapped up in him she can't see the wood for the trees. Maybe the best thing would be for Ricky and me to leave Walford. It's the only other option. I sent off my application to Brighton and a few other colleges, but I ain't heard nothing back, yet. I ain't holding my breath – I mean, I ain't got a single GCSE, what hope have I got? – but there's always Frank's list of contacts. If Ricky could get a job somewhere else, that would be a start, and then I could sort something out once we'd got ourselves settled.

I can't go on like this. I'll go crazy. We've gotta have our own place, and there ain't been a sniff of one round here. Ricky says I'm always in a mood these days, and no wonder, living here. I nearly killed Janine today after I found her going through my stuff – personal things, like old letters. She had even been using my make-up. I told Ricky it was the last straw, I want us to leave, but I know he ain't thrilled about it. He likes having his family all around him. Tough. It's in his own best interests too, if only he knew it.

6 July

Nat's the only person I can talk to these days. Ricky don't see what my problem is – he reckons Janine can do no wrong – and Peggy's playing the interfering mother-in-law, criticizing everything I do with Liam. I know she thinks she's helping, but I wish she'd just back off. It's hard enough to cope with the broken nights – I can hardly keep me eyes open at work – without having Peggy banging on about how we're too soft with Liam and we shouldn't be taking him into our bed. I just want someone to tell me I'm doing alright with my baby. I wish Tiff was here, she went through all this with Peggy and Courtney.

Nat said I should talk to Mum and not be put off by Dan, so in the end that was what I did. I went over there at lunchtime, hoping to catch Mum by herself, but Dan opened the door in his dressing-gown and it was pretty clear what they'd just been up to. I couldn't cope with that, so I said it wasn't important and shot off. I was practically running out the gate.

I know it's daft – I never had any hang-ups over Mum and Alan's sex life – but this is different. This is … personal. Too personal. The stupidest thing is, I feel … well, jealous, I suppose. Crazy, innit? Not cos Mum's got Dan, I ain't that pathetic, no way! Can't think why I ever fancied a wrinkly like him in the first place. No, it's because that part of my life has gone down the plughole. The last time me and Ricky made love was in Southend, just before I met Dan. Before that we hadn't done it that much – it's too difficult, with Liam in the cot next to us, he always wakes up at the crucial moment – and since Southend we ain't done it at all. I'm always too tired or stressed out these days. If Ricky tries it on, I just bark at him. I know I shouldn't, but I can't help it. I've gone right off having sex with him.

Living with the rest of the Butchers don't help. Even if I was up for it, I couldn't do it with Peggy and Frank in the next room. Me and Ricky were supposed to be talking about moving after we'd got Liam off tonight, but we never got the chance, what with Ricky running round at Janine's beck and call. Then I found him giving her money and I hit the roof! Here we are, saving to get our own place, and Ricky's handing out cash to Janine like he's giving her sweets. Anyway, she answered me back, so I told her to keep out of it and she started howling like a baby. Honestly, she screams louder than Liam! Peggy stuck her oar in and I ended up telling them both exactly what I thought of them.

I ain't sorry for what I said. Janine's had it coming and Peggy never knows when to stop. I told her straight, I was sick and tired of her going on at me about Liam. I mean, like her kids turned out so perfect! Great examples of child-rearing, Phil and Grant are. Course, that put Peggy's back up and she went, 'If that's how you feel, why don't you find somewhere else to live?' Like I ain't desperate enough to get out, as it is! I hate the whole lot of 'em.

8 July

We've moved. Just hope it's not out of the frying pan and into the fire. We're at number 25 with Mum, Dan, Robbie and Sonia. I couldn't stick it in the Vic another second, not after this evening. I'd been at Mum's – Ricky said she wanted to see me – and when I got back to the Vic I found out why he was so keen for me to go over there. I'd been got out of the way, in case I spoiled the Butchers' little gathering of the clans.

I could hear people laughing as I came up the stairs, and when I walked into the lounge they was all sitting round the big table – Peggy, Frank, Ricky, Janine, Grant, Phil, Jamie and Courtney – drinking Champagne and eating birthday cake. The place went silent and Ricky jumped up looking dead nervous. He said it was a surprise party for Grant's birthday but it was obvious it wasn't just some last-minute thing. I felt so humiliated. Talk about making it clear I wasn't wanted. If they'd hung up a sign saying 'Bog off, Bianca' it couldn't have been more obvious.

Everyone started being all super-polite, like, 'Oh, do have some cake, Bianca', 'Come and sit here, Bianca', when all I wanted was for the floor to open up and swallow me. Frank had the grace to look a bit embarrassed and even Grant looked awkward, but Janine was loving every moment. Then Peggy started on again about Liam's sleeping habits and that just about finished me off. I mumbled something about not feeling hungry and dashed out. Ricky came chasing after me, blathering excuses, but I was in no mood to listen and started packing our stuff up, slinging it all into carrier-bags and suitcases. I told him Liam and I were leaving, and he could choose whether he wanted to go back to the next room and play happy families or be with his own.

A couple of hours later, the three of us had moved in at Mum's. Dan was pretty shaken when he saw us – I don't think she'd told him about inviting us to stay – but that's his lookout.

I ain't making it easy for him. He'll have to like it or lump it. I don't wanna be here any more than he wants me here, but for the moment I ain't got no choice. We'll just have to keep out of each other's way, that's all.

12 July

I don't know what's happening to me. I can't relax, can't eat, can't sleep. Living here's a nightmare. It's almost as cramped as the Vic, and the atmosphere's ten times as tense. Well, it is between me and Dan. We can't even pass the milk without it being a loaded gesture. Everywhere I go, he's in my face. I'm aware of him wherever he is in the house. It's so intense, it's like a forcefield between us.

Sitting next to him on the sofa this evening, I was surprised no-one else could sense it. It was like static, like when you take something out of the dryer and it crackles and your skin feels all prickly. I could actually feel the hairs standing up on the back of my neck. We sat there watching telly until everyone else had gone up to bed (Ricky had gone off to the pub in a strop). Neither of us said anything. We didn't even speak to each other. I was holding my breath, wondering what he would do. It was like we were both playing a waiting game, each one trying to see how long before the other one cracks.

Nothing happened, of course. I don't know what I was expecting. Perhaps I'm imagining it. When I look at Dan, it's hard to know what's real and what's in my mind. I go over our conversations afterwards and tear them apart for hidden meanings, even though we hardly talk, all we do is fight. All sorts of crazy things have been going round in my head, these last few days. Things I don't want to think about. All I know is, the sooner Dan's out of our lives, the better, not just for Mum, for me and Ricky, too.

I can't help drawing comparisons, when I see Dan and Ricky together. Dan's such a man, and Ricky's such a boy. There's

something about Dan's body – it's so tall and hard and powerful – that gives me butterflies when I look at him. I feel terrible
for admitting that. For being so disloyal. I keep telling myself
it's natural, given how it used to be with me and Dan. The
chemistry between us was something else. As for the sex, it was
the best I've ever had. Nobody else has ever come close. But sex
ain't everything, I've learned that the hard way. It's a quick fix,
not a long-term solution. A good steady marriage is far more
important, especially when you've got a family. Me and Ricky
are just going through a bad patch. Things will pick up again
when we've got our own place.

13 July

Who am I kidding? I think I'm in love with Dan.

There. I can't believe I've said it. Thank God for this diary.
I'd go mental if I couldn't get it all out somehow. I'm having to
keep it hidden in a shoebox under the bed and I write it when
Ricky's not about. No-one can ever know. And I can't ever do
anything about it, that's the worst thing. I've been fighting the
feeling from the minute I clapped eyes on him in Southend, but
it was only tonight that I finally realized what it was. I've been
so caught up in a whirl of emotions about Mum and Dan and
me and Ricky that I couldn't see what was staring me in the
face. Literally.

I felt so let down this morning when I got up, and I couldn't
think why. Or, at least, I didn't want to admit to myself why.
But the truth was, I wanted Dan to make a pass at me last
night, when we was sitting by ourselves on the sofa, and he
didn't. A few years ago we'd have been all over each other. It
was like I'd failed some kind of test, I wasn't attractive no
more. My ex fancies my Mum more than me. That's a real
boost, that is.

I guess I've let meself go a bit, since I've had Liam. I don't
get the chance to dress up these days. No point, is there?

When do me and Ricky go anywhere? I've been slouching round the market in me old clothes, hair all scraped back, not bothering with make-up. Not exactly a pretty sight. I know I need a bit of slap to look presentable, but I've been past caring lately.

I thought, maybe that's why Dan didn't go for me. Then, today, I found meself dressing really carefully, trying on all different clothes, 'stead of grabbing the first thing that falls out the wardrobe. I washed my hair and let it dry loose and put some lippy and mascara on. I was determined to get him to notice me. When I came downstairs he was on the phone and he turned round and looked at me and there was something in his eyes – well, I thought there was, for a second – and I thought, yeah, he ain't so cool, he feels it too, but he was really curt and we ended up spitting nails at each other, as usual.

Dan asked me to give Mum a message to say he couldn't make their lunch date, but I told him he could do his own dirty work. He wrote her a note and left it on the hall table, but it fell face down when he went out. I thought, I'm blowed if I'm gonna turn that over. I mean, it ain't my responsibility!

I saw Mum later when me and Nat was having our sandwiches on the bench by the War Memorial. She was well hacked off about Dan not turning up. I said, 'Two weeks of living together and he's letting you down already.' Afterwards, Natalie said I shouldn't meddle but I told her, I'm trying to protect Mum. I think Nat's seen through me, though. She told me I was jealous. I told her what she could do with her opinion and walked off, but it frightened me to hear it from someone else. It was like I couldn't ignore it any longer.

Then, this evening, me and Dan had this moment together that blew my mind. Ricky and I had gone out to look at flats – total waste of time, they were dumps, all of them – and when we got back he went straight upstairs to check on Liam and I went to make us a cup of tea. I walked into the kitchen and there was Dan, lighting some candles at the table. It was all laid for a romantic meal for two and there was soft music going, so I knew he was trying to get back into Mum's good books. He came over to me and said, 'What exactly is your problem?' and I said, 'Oh, it's perfectly normal, all this, innit? You and me living here in the same house, keeping our little secret buried like it never even happened.'

He said, 'It's gone, it's in the past', and I said, 'No, it ain't, cos you're right here, in my face, every day'. I went to go out, but he grabbed hold of my arm and pulled me right up close. Our faces were that near I could feel his breath on my cheek. He was breathing fast and his fingers were digging into my skin. He whispered, 'What do you want, Bianca?' and his eyes were burning into me. I could feel myself trembling and I knew then that what I wanted most in the world was for him to kiss me. It was like everything was spinning out of control. I wanted Dan so bad, I ached. To be in his arms, crushed against his chest, to smell his skin, taste his kiss … the feeling was almost unbearable.

I tried to get a grip, but it was so hard. My eyes started welling up and I said, 'I can't do this any more. It's doing my head in. I don't want to lie to my own mum about something like this'. He took my chin in his hand and forced me to look at him, and for a split second I thought he was gonna kiss me, but instead he said, 'We've never lied to her. We're in too deep, what good would it do, telling her now?'

I knew it would do one thing. It would put a stop to this craziness before anything happened. It would save me. It might save us all. I said, 'She's got to know the truth, Dan. If you don't tell her, I will.' And this time I really meant it. I pulled away from him and ran out the kitchen. I was shaking so much I could hardly climb the stairs. I had to lock myself in the bathroom and stuff a hanky in my mouth to stop Ricky from hearing me crying.

My birthday. I can safely say it's been the worst birthday ever in my life. My husband's left me, my mum threw me out, everyone in the Square hates me – oh yeah, and I snogged my ex-boyfriend. Who's just decided to marry my mum. Did I leave anything out?

It's 2 a.m., and Ricky still ain't come home, so I guess he's staying at the Vic tonight. He cleared off after I let rip at him. I don't blame him, I said some awful things. I just lost it with everybody. They should never have sprung a surprise party on me. The last thing I wanted was to be in the limelight, especially with a load of people who have to be rounded up and dragged here with the offer of free booze. I know how people see me – ratty old loud-mouth – but at least I speak the truth. Well, I used to, anyway. Before Dan.

I'd been getting more and more wound up all evening. Dan came into the bathroom when I was getting ready to go out – I thought Ricky was taking me for a romantic dinner – and when I asked if he'd told Mum about us, he said he hadn't. I gave him an ultimatum: do it tonight, or I will. After we'd gone out, I wished I hadn't. The thought of not having Dan around was worse than the agony of having him around. I had this sudden horror of me and Ricky growing old together, and it made me feel panicky inside, like, is this all my life's ever going to amount to?

It didn't help that Ricky took us to this disgusting kebab house. And with me dolled up to the nines in a slinky new dress, expecting to be wined and dined! Course, it was all just pretend so that he could get me out of the house – it was all a big joke to Ricky and he was playing it up, ordering donas and chips, and then pretending he'd lost his wallet. I just burst into tears. I couldn't bear it. I thought, I'm twenty-two and I'm stuck with this loser, while the man I really want is about to leave me again, for ever.

We had to go back to the house – for the wallet, supposedly – and when I walked into the front room to look for it, everyone shouted 'surprise' and threw party-poppers over me. I nearly jumped out of my skin. I was feeling so miserable and it was the hardest thing in the world to scrape on a smile and pretend I was enjoying myself. I tried, but I just couldn't. Especially when I saw Dan was still there.

It was obvious he hadn't said anything to Mum. She was draped round his neck, dancing with him, a silly smile all over her face. I dragged Ricky into the room to dance, and put on a show for Dan, moving my hips to the rhythm, and really getting into it. I gave him a look under my eyelashes to wind him up. Dan couldn't take his eyes off my body. I could feel him watching, his stare scorching into me, but then he walked off and as soon as he did all the energy I'd had drained right out of me.

I followed him out and we had another set-to, which made me feel even worse. I was about to go and hide myself away with Liam when Mum caught up with me and asked what was wrong. I said, 'You wouldn't want to know,' and she said, 'You always had your little secrets, didn't you?' I thought, it's now or never, I've got to tell her about me and Dan cos he's not gonna, so I said, 'I still do'. Then she said, 'Join the club. I got one right now. Want to hear it?'

I went, 'Want to hear mine?', but Mum got in first. She said it was about Dan, which stalled me and I lost the moment. Then she said he'd asked her to marry him and she'd said yes. I just stood there, feeling as if I'd been stabbed through the heart. Mum was so full of it, she didn't even ask me what my secret was. She went off all giggly like a schoolgirl. I saw Dan looking up at me from the bottom of the stairs and I rushed off into the bedroom. I thought I was gonna be physically sick.

I was gonna plead a headache and stay up there, but Sonia dragged me down to the kitchen to cut the cake. I had to endure everyone singing 'Happy Birthday' to me, then Mum made a speech and blabbed her precious little secret to the entire room. Everyone was congratulating her and I couldn't take it any more. I said, 'Go on, then, marry him, make a fool of yourself,' and Peggy butted in all sarky, 'Oh dear, she's off'. I shouted, 'You can shut up an' all', and then I couldn't stop myself. All this bitterness came pouring out and I went for the whole lot of them, telling them they was all a load of hypocrites and to clear off.

That was when me and Ricky bust up. He hauled me into the front room and said he couldn't take much more, and I went, 'Then don't. Give up, walk out on me, I don't care.' I wanted him to hate me. I said, 'You're like a little puppy dog. I kick you. You run back for more.' Only this time he didn't. He said he knew I didn't love him and even if we moved to the North Pole it wouldn't change anything. Poor Ricky. He's right. It's me that can't admit it. Even when he was slamming out the door, I tried to stop him, tell him I did love him really. He said, 'No, Bianca, you don't. I may be thick but I know what love is. And this ain't it.'

Course Mum was steaming by then and she and I had a mega-row in front of Dan, Sonia and Robbie. We both had our claws out and it got really vicious and she accused me of being jealous of her happiness. I so nearly told her the truth, but, when it came to it, I couldn't. I said Dan was gonna hurt her like she'd never been hurt before, only she was too stubborn or too stupid to see it. That was when she slapped me across the face and told me to get out of the house. Sonia was crying and Robbie was white, and even Dan looked shocked. He took her off to the Vic and I was left all alone in the kitchen, shaking from head to foot.

Dan came back ten minutes later, just as I was packing to go. I didn't know where to, a hotel or somewhere. Just out of that house, away from Dan, away from all the pain. He asked me to stay, and I said, 'Why? Wanna watch me suffer some more, do you?' I told him, every time I see him I'm reminded of the time he dumped me and left me crying in that pub. Then he said it weren't that easy for him, and if I hadn't been so young and he hadn't been married, he would never have let me go.

My heart started to beat faster, and I said, 'You don't mean that', cos I could hardly believe my ears. He said, 'I do', and I knew then there was hope. We were caught in one of those moments that change your life. You say one thing, it goes one way, you don't say it and it goes in the opposite direction. So I said it. Took a deep breath and came out with the truth. 'I was mad about you, Dan. I loved you … still do.'

Even then, I had a chance to turn back. Just at that moment, Ricky hammered on the door, shouting my name. I was gonna answer him, but Dan put his arm out and stopped me.

We stood there in silence and Ricky went away. Then Dan said he felt the same way as me. I couldn't breathe. He pulled me towards him and told me he loved me and even though I knew it was wrong, I couldn't resist. We stared into each other's eyes and it was like I'd come home, at last. I kissed him on the lips and he held me close and suddenly we were devouring each other like animals. I could hear myself saying, 'I love you, Dan, I love you, I love you', and my voice seemed to be coming from far away. He lifted me on to the kitchen table and pulled up my dress and I didn't care, I just wanted him there, then, inside me. Then there was the sound of the front door opening and Mum called out, 'Dan? Bianca?' and we both froze.

Dan started to pull away, but I wouldn't let him go. I just couldn't. I wasn't thinking, I was on autopilot. I clung on to him like a limpet, refusing to give him up. I didn't care any more. I wanted Mum to find us, see the truth with her own eyes. Dan was mine, not hers. He always had been and he always would be.

But Dan wouldn't do it. He twisted his arm round my shoulder, making it look like he was comforting me, so when Mum came in, she thought I was crying on his shoulder. Which I was. I heard Mum say, 'What's going on?' and Dan went, 'It's OK. Everything's all right now. We've had a little chat and things have calmed down. Haven't they, Bianca?' It was like I'd lost all control. I felt so weak, after what had just happened. I gave in, played it his way, let Dan do the talking. I just didn't have the fight left to stick the knife in.

I said yes. Mum and me ended up hugging and I said I was sorry and she rocked me in her arms like a child and said, 'It's all right now, baby, everything's gonna be OK'. Dan was standing behind her, staring right at me. I couldn't read his expression. I'm so confused now. I don't know how things stand. Who does he want, Mum ... or me?

18 July

My life's a hopeless mess. I didn't sleep at all last night. I was writing 'til morning, trying to get things straight in my head, but I ended up more confused than ever. I left the house really early to set up the stall, cos I couldn't face anyone. Especially not Mum. And I was afraid of seeing Dan and hearing him say our kiss was all a mistake and it shouldn't have happened.

When I did see him – he followed me into the caff – it turned out that was what he was expecting me to say. Then he said he was glad it had happened, and my heart skipped a beat, but I tried not to show anything. I said, 'We can't talk here,' cos Robbie was watching us from the counter, and Dan said to meet him at the allotments at four o'clock.

I spent the whole day trying to decide whether to turn up or not, but I couldn't make up my mind. Dan was hanging around the Square, like he was keeping an eye on me, but I kept avoiding him. I was torn between feeling guilty about Ricky and wanting to be with Dan. By five-to-four, I still hadn't decided, but then Mum came over to the stall and offered to look after Liam so I could go and see Ricky and make it up with him. I felt terrible. She was just handing me this opportunity on a plate. I kept saying no, it's alright, but she insisted – although I almost gave the game away by heading off in the opposite direction to the Arches. I had to pretend I was going there, then double back down Bridge Street when Mum wasn't looking.

I did go to the allotments. I saw Dan sitting on a bench waiting for me. I still wasn't sure what I was gonna do or say, or even why I had come. I hung back, watching him, trying to decide. Last night was one thing. I was out of control, but I knew if I went along with Dan this time, it'd be a different thing altogether. That was what finally focused my mind. I thought, what are you getting yourself into, Bianca? You ain't footloose and fancy free, you've got a baby to think about. How can you do this to Liam? And what about Ricky?

I mean, even if Ricky don't ring my bell, he's a good father and a good husband. He won't let us down. He might get things wrong sometimes, but he always tries. I remembered what he said to me last night – 'Every day I try to please you' – and he does. I've been so hard on him, knocking him back all the time. I thought, Mum's right, I am a selfish little cow. I've been all caught up in my own feelings without thinking about the consequences. I've got to be sensible for Liam's sake.

I left without Dan seeing me and went round to the Arches. Ricky was sitting on a chair staring into a mug of tea, looking really down. I said, 'I'm so sorry', and burst into tears and he came over at once and held me. I was pathetically grateful and wept buckets into his shirt. He was so familiar, and safe. We went back to the house and kissed and made up and I told him I loved him (which I do – not in a mad, passionate way, but we do have a deep bond). He said, 'You hurt me. Don't ever do that again – I couldn't take it', and I promised I wouldn't. I know what I've decided now.

I wanted us to leave then and there, pack our bags and go to a hotel, get away from Dan and Mum. Of course, I couldn't put it like that, so it didn't make sense to Ricky. He said it would use up our savings and it wouldn't be fair to Liam and we'd have to stick it out for a bit longer until we could get our own place. My heart sank, but what could I say? We went upstairs and I let Ricky make love to me, but all I could think of was Dan. I kept trying to imagine Ricky was Dan, but it didn't work. I don't think Ricky noticed. He was just happy we was together again. Me, I've never been so miserable in my life. I feel totally and utterly cornered.

20 July

I'm sticking to my decision, but it's so hard. Dan and I are sniping at each other, both of us trying to prove that we don't need each other. I wonder who we're fooling? If anything, it's made the situation between us even more tense.

He came round to the stall this morning, asking where I got to yesterday. Said he waited forty-five minutes for me at the allotments. I said, 'Something else came up. My husband. Not that it's any business of yours.' Then he asked me again if I'd really meant what I said on Saturday night. I said, 'You waited forty-five minutes and I never showed up? There's your answer.'

It felt good to put the boot in at the time, give him back some of what he's given me, but afterwards I felt worse than ever. I did mean it, when we kissed. I do love Dan. It's just that I love Ricky, too. It's a different kind of love. My love for Dan is, like, off-the-scale passion, whereas Ricky is more like a best friend. We've done a lot of growing up together, me and Ricky. He's helped me through some really bad times and we've come out the other side stronger for it. Or so I thought, anyway. All this with Dan has taken me by surprise. I wasn't looking for anyone else. Now I've discovered a side to me that I'd almost forgotten existed and I'm having to battle every second of the day not to give in to it. I'm trying to do what my head tells me, not what my heart tells me, but it's tearing me apart. I've decided that the only option is to make sure me and Dan are never alone together, that way I won't be vulnerable.

It's easier said than done, though. He came chasing after me up Bridge Street this evening when I popped out to the First 'til Last to get some milk. I kept walking, but he tried to stop me with some pathetic comment about Liam. I said it was a cheap shot and headed for the house, but he put his hand on my arm and tried to stop me. The touch of his fingers on my skin was like a jolt of electricity. I can cope if he keeps his distance, but when he touches me … It was all I could do to get through the front door without collapsing into his arms.

22 July

Got a rejection letter from one of the colleges I applied to. I'm trying to stay positive – I applied to loads – but Ricky seems to think that's the end of it. I don't know. It's so difficult to think about the future. Just making it through each day is hard enough at the moment. Ricky's started house-hunting and we've got piles of stuff from estate agents, so I'm sure something will come up. But it'd better happen soon. Dan's pursuing me and this evening I nearly gave in to him.

I was by myself, waiting for Ricky to get home and Dan came in. I asked if he'd seen Ricky and he said he wouldn't be back 'til late cos he was doing some rush job for Phil. I knew then that I'd been set up and I went to walk out of the room, but Dan tried to stop me. He said we needed to talk about what had happened at the party. I told him I was drunk and that all the things I'd said didn't mean a thing. He said, 'I don't buy that, because that would make you a tease. Are you a tease, Bianca?' When I said no, he said, 'Then you did mean it, didn't you?'

Dan was really close to me, looking down into my eyes. His shirt was unbuttoned at the top and I could feel the heat of his body, smell his bare skin. I recognized his aftershave – a really musky male scent that used to drive me wild – and all of a sudden I wanted to rip the buttons off his shirt and slide my hands inside. He said, 'Believe me, it would be easier to pretend last week and before never happened. But I can't. All I can think about is you. Your hair, your skin, your lips...'

I groaned, 'Don't. Please. We can't do this', but he bent his head towards me until our mouths were only inches apart and whispered, 'We can do whatever we want'. I felt my stomach flip over. My voice came out in a croak. 'You're going to marry my mum. And I'm already married. We can't.'

He said, 'And is that what you want?' His eyes were shining, unblinking, totally focused on mine. I felt as if I was being drawn towards them, as if they were reeling me in. I managed to say, 'It doesn't matter what I want', but Dan knew I didn't mean it. He traced my cheek with his finger and I stood stock still, letting him do it. Then he lifted my chin towards him and stroked my lips with his thumb. It was like, this is a hint of what you could have, and it set me on fire. I told him I wanted him to leave me alone and he said, 'No, you don't'. I don't know how long we stood like that, just staring into each other's eyes. Time seemed to just stop. I wasn't me, any more, I had let go of right and wrong and reason. I was just reacting, feeling, being.

The front door slammed and we were both jolted out of the moment. We pulled apart a split second before Ricky came into the room. He didn't seem to notice anything, just wanted to know what was for tea. I managed to put on a bright smile and said I'd go and see what we had. Ricky went, 'What about you?' to Dan, and Dan looked at me and said, 'I'm fine. I can wait.' It gave me a secret thrill. We both knew exactly what he meant.

26 July

Thank God Ricky came in when he did. I didn't think that last night, but now I see it in the cold light of day, I'm glad things didn't go no further. It's just so hard to keep a lid on my emotions when Dan's around. He's got the knack of stirring me up, he knows how to press my buttons. I'm just gonna have to try harder to stay out of his company.

At least he weren't around this evening. Mind you, neither was Ricky. They both went off to play snooker with Grant and Phil. I was cross cos Ricky forgot to say anything about it to me. Besides, I didn't like the thought of those two going out together, talking about me behind my back. I don't trust Dan to play fair.

It meant Mum and I had a cosy little night in – not! I can't stand hearing her going on about Dan and how wonderful he is. I was hoping that when she went over to see Alan, they might have patched things up – stupid hope, I know. Who said love was about logic? If it was, I'd have handled this Dan thing completely differently. It's so hard to do the right thing when all your senses are screaming at you to do the wrong one...

27 July

I'm coping, but only by freezing Dan out completely. We're living on a knife edge. Just passing each other in the kitchen is a major trauma. If he so much as brushes my arm, I get goosebumps all over. Sometimes, I want him so much I feel faint. Watching him doing stupid little things, like washing-up ... his strong wrists, the dark hairs on his arm, his big hands all soapy. Pathetic, innit? I'm obsessed.

Even though I'm doing my best to ignore Dan, I can't take my eyes off him and he can't take his eyes off me. Today I was walking along Bridge Street and I knew he was close by, even before I spotted him, because I could feel his eyes boring into me. I turned round and there he was, outside the First 'til Last, just staring at me. It was almost spooky. He tried to get me on my own this evening, said we had to sort ourselves out. I said, 'When are you gonna get it into your head? I'm not gonna talk about it, ever.'

Trying to act normal for the sake of Mum and Ricky is a nightmare. Ricky's getting the brunt of my frustration, as always. I'm being a right bitch to him. He's into this house-hunting in a big way now. 'Settle down' seem to be the only two words he knows. Thing is, I can't get enthusiastic about it, even though I know I should. I need to get away from Dan, and the sooner the better, but I can't bear the thought of not being near to him. It's all such a mess and I can't see a way out.

29 July

I feel so weird. Kind of light-headed and reckless, as if I could do anything. It's like I've crossed a line into the danger zone. I ought to be scared, I ought to be sorry, but I'm not. I'm walk-ing on air. Why? Because I've slept with Dan. At last.

I didn't plan it. But he did. I've been making an effort to avoid him, but he set up a trap and I walked right into it. I had my doubts when Ricky first told me that Dan knew of a place for sale. It was a flat in Bow, private sale for a mate of his – nice location, not far from here, affordable, no agency fees – almost too good to be true. I thought that at the time, but I didn't twig on to him then. It wasn't until I found out he hadn't mentioned it to Mum that I got suspicious. Especially when the viewing was at a time Ricky couldn't make. I nearly didn't go at all, but Mum was nagging me to see it and I couldn't find an excuse to get out of it. Well, I probably could have, if I'd tried hard enough, but I was intrigued.

I kept telling myself, you're imagining all this, Dan's not that scheming, but when I knocked on the door, it was Dan who opened it. Even though I was half-expecting it, it was still a shock to find out I was right. I was furious and tried to walk away but he got hold of my shoulders and held on to me so I couldn't move. I told him I wasn't interested, but he said I couldn't just head home and tell the others the house wasn't even for sale, so in the end I went inside.

I told him the situation was impossible, but he said, 'Won't go away, though, will it? Not something as powerful as this.' He told me there was no point fighting it because we couldn't help how we felt, and that made sense, sort of. I was so tired of battling to resist him, it was a relief to think, yeah, why not? Live for the moment. I've been wanting Dan like mad for so long and I dream about being with him all the time. Every night I lie awake, fantasizing about making love with him. I've already been unfaithful to Ricky in my head. And not just in my head. I've kissed Dan. I've told him I love him. I mean, is it such a big step to take off your clothes and go all the way?

It felt dead strange being in someone else's flat, but in a way it added to the excitement. We sat down on the sofa and Dan stroked my arm and I felt my skin tingle all over. I looked into his eyes and knew I wasn't gonna back down this time. It was like nothing in the whole world mattered at that moment except him and me. I leant forward and kissed him hard on the lips. He broke it off and stared into my face, like he was check-ing I really meant it. It made me feel angry and vulnerable, cos I thought he was winding me up or something, but then he grabbed me and pulled me against him and I stopped thinking and just let my body take over. It was the most incredible sex I've ever had, better than when we were seeing each other last time. I'm more experienced now, I know what I want, and Dan was fantastic. It's like up 'til now I've been going round half-asleep and now I know what it's like to be really alive.

30 July

I can't believe the way I'm behaving. And the risks I'm taking. Just writing this is risky enough in itself – I can't bear to think about what would happen if anyone found it. I have to write it when Ricky's asleep. I couldn't sleep a wink anyway last night after being with Dan, and he couldn't, either. We ended up snogging in the bathroom first thing this morning, before everybody else got up. We would've gone a lot further, too, if it hadn't been for Liam crying and waking the entire household. He's got some front, Dan has. I don't know how he can do the things he does to me and then act so normal with Mum. I got really upset at breakfast, seeing her all lovey-dovey with him. I just had to get away from them. It was so hard to stomach when only half an hour earlier I'd been in Dan's arms.

I was in a right old state, especially when Ricky started asking about the flat. I told him it wouldn't suit us, then Ricky said he finished work earlier than he thought yesterday and nearly made it over there! His exact words were, 'I wish I'd seen it – I nearly caught you' – which made me go hot and cold all over. I rushed off to open the stall without my moneybelt, but at least it gave Dan an excuse to follow me out. He said he wanted to see me today and he wasn't leaving until we'd agreed something. (I like the way he stands up to me, it's so different from Ricky!) In the end we arranged to meet in the allotments at one o'clock and I promised that, this time, I'd be there.

Course, I'd forgotten Liam was only doing a half-day at his nursery and I was supposed to pick him up at one. Mum reminded me later and I was going frantic trying to fix things up. Finally I got Teresa to cover for me on the stall and persuaded Nat to have Liam. I raced round to the allotments, cos I didn't want Dan to think I was standing him up again, and we fell into each other's arms. We were kissing on a bench like a couple of teenagers and then he said, 'I've been waiting all morning to do that,' which made my heart go all fluttery. I asked Dan if he liked being with me more than Mum, but he wouldn't give me a straight answer, then he asked if I loved Ricky, and I said I wasn't sure. That brought us crashing down to earth again. I'm fine when it's just the two of us, but as soon as I start thinking about the practicalities, I feel really depressed.

Afterwards, I felt bad about dumping Liam on Nat – she ain't babysat him before and she don't know the first thing about babies. I thought, what am I doing, palming off my own child like that? But at the time I was so desperate to see Dan, it was all I could focus on. Anyway, Nat seemed to enjoy herself and Liam survived OK. I bought Nat a drink later and she said it had made her feel quite broody. I told her, 'You don't want to rush into having kids and end up tying yourself down. Have some fun first.' I mean, it's not that I'm regretting Liam, cos I love him to bits, it's just that I'm beginning to realize how narrow my world's become...

3 August

The stress of all this is really beginning to get to me. I woke up with a splitting headache and I ain't been able to shake it off all day. Had to nip home for some painkillers and I was just taking them when Dan walked in. He wanted me to shut the stall early and spend the afternoon with him. I told him he'd bankrupt me at this rate, but I said yes. I can't refuse him. It's getting out of control. We arranged to meet outside the Tube at two, but then Mum came home and we couldn't talk any more.

It all got really complicated because Ricky found me later and told me he'd fixed up for us to look at this showhouse on some new estate at two o'clock. I tried to get him to change the day, but he got shirty with me and thought I couldn't be bothered, so in the end I said yes just to shut him up. I wasn't gonna go – I thought I'd come up with some excuse later – but as I was getting ready to meet Dan, it suddenly hit me what a lying, deceitful cow I've become. I was tarting myself up, putting on make-up, and I suddenly caught sight of Liam's teddy in the mirror. I just went to pieces. I thought, I'm not only betraying my husband and my mother, I'm betraying my own son, and it flashed through my mind all that stuff I'd said to Louise about betraying Simon and Tiff. I thought, that's it, I'm no better than her. It was such a shock. I mean, what Louise did was unforgivable … am I really in the same league?

I tried to convince myself that I'm not. At least Dan and me have got a history. I mean, none of this would've happened otherwise. I started thinking back to when me and Dan was together, first time around, and I remembered some photos somebody took of us at a party. I hid them inside the cover of one of my schoolbooks. I started looking through my stuff and eventually I found them. It was so weird seeing us together then. We look so young! Well, I was just a schoolgirl, and even though Dan was thirty-three, he had more hair and less lines than he's got now. Sometimes I wonder if I dreamt it all up, what happened between us, but we look so happy in those photos, not a care in the world. It really brought it all back.

I forgot all about the time, and when I heard footsteps on the stairs, it made me jump out of my skin. I only just got the photos hidden before Mum came into my room. Can't think how I'd have explained that one if she'd seen them! Dan was right behind her, cos he was looking for me, then Ricky turned up, too, wondering if I was all right. I told them all I'd got a thumping headache and wanted to be left alone. After that, I crawled under the duvet and stayed there for the rest of the day. I just wanted to curl up somewhere warm and safe and dark and not face up to the world.

4 August

Still got a headache. At least that ain't a lie. I may be telling Ricky plenty of others, but my excuse for not having sex with him is genuine. Well, partly. Truth is, I can't bear him to touch me. He keeps trying it on and I don't want to know. I can't help it. All I can think about is Dan and how much I love him. I love him so much that nothing else matters. Not when I'm with him, anyway. When I can't see him or be with him, I'm dead miserable. The stall's losing money, my marriage is going down the drain, and I'm here, moping around like a schoolgirl. Just like the schoolgirl who first met Dan, in fact. I keep thinking, if only we hadn't split up then, everything would be easy. I really don't think I could cope if I lost him again.

Dan came back to the house this afternoon, and found me here. We took a chance and kissed and cuddled on the sofa. It felt so good just to be close to him again. Things got pretty steamy and he wanted us to go upstairs and make love, but I couldn't. I can't do it in my mother's house, it ain't right. Whose bed would we do it in, for a start? My Mum's? Mine and Ricky's? It's impossible. I can't switch off and forget about everything, however much I want Dan. I told him that and he said we could borrow his mate's flat again, but I don't know. It's all so underhand, all this sneaking around and lying. I hate it. I've always prided myself on being honest and truthful and I've always demanded it in my relationships, and here I am, carrying on like the worst of them. I'm beginning to think it would be better to bring it all out in the open, however bad the consequences. I just don't want to lie any more.

9 August

Dan's away on a business trip. He wanted me to go with him, but I said no. I can't just drop everything and, anyway, I couldn't abandon Liam like that. But I'm missing him like crazy. He rang the caff today to talk to Mum and I answered it, and it was such a rush to hear his voice. He said he wished I was there with him and then Mum asked who it was, so I had to hand the phone over. I could tell he was saying suggestive things to her from the way she was giggling and telling him he had a dirty mind. It ties my stomach in knots when he does that. I had to rush out of the caff.

I keep asking myself, does he get some sort of kick out of it, stringing along mother and daughter? I mean, talk about having your cake and eating it ... when I ask him who he really wants, he ducks the question, but then he tells me how he spends all night thinking about me when he's with Mum ... I mean, it's gotta be me. If it wasn't, why would he put us both through this? I'm pretty certain who he'd choose if I laid it on the line. It's me that's hanging back. I'm the one with everything to lose. The reason I don't do it is because I can't bear to hurt Mum. It would be kinder to Ricky, really, cos I know I'm making him unhappy. But then I'd be depriving Liam of his father, and Ricky's so good with him ... it's all such a mess. The guilt kicks in at every turn. I don't know how much longer I can keep this up. Sooner or later, something's got to give.

10 August

I've got an interview for a fashion course. The letter came today – it's from Manchester. I'd begun to forget about all that, to be honest. I've had three rejection letters already, including one from Brighton, and with everything else that's been going on, I've pushed it to the back of my mind. I wasn't even that excited when I got the news, whereas a few weeks ago I'd've been over the moon. I just can't get my mind around anything in the future until me and Dan sort things out.

Found Mum crying in the kitchen this afternoon. My blood ran cold for a second, cos I thought she must have found out, somehow, but then she said she was just a bit upset because she was missing Dan, especially at the moment. I asked her why now, and she said it was because of Billy's custody hearing – Alan's going for an interim custody order until he can get full custody – and it was making her stressed out. She asked me to give her a hug, and I did, but I felt like Judas.

PS. Dan got back this evening. I was in the living room with Mum, trying on trendy clothes for my college interview when he came in. We didn't hear him at first. I had on this dress that finished just below me bum and I was striking silly poses, and I suddenly felt Dan looking at me. He didn't say nothing, just stood there, watching me, undressing me with his eyes. Then Mum saw him and rushed into his arms and I had to go out because that was where I wanted to be, more than anywhere else in the world.

12 August

Ricky dragged me out to Essex at lunchtime, to have a look round this showhouse he's been banging on about. It was one of them new estates where all the houses look the same, except you get the choice of six colour schemes. Big deal! We had this Essex wideboy show us round. He really got on my nerves with his smarmy sales talk. Ricky was raving about the house, going on about how he could turn the garage into a workshop and Liam would be able to ride his bike outside and Mum and Dan could come over to stay at weekends. The more he went on about it, the more the whole idea stuck in my throat, especially when he started talking about having a swing in the garden for 'the kids'.

Afterwards, he tried to get me to go for a drive with him to Epping Forest. Well, I knew what that meant, and it wasn't scenery he was interested in! I made some excuse about needing to see a wholesaler in Bethnal Green, but really I had to get to Dan's mate's flat in Bow. Dan and I had arranged to meet there and he'd given me a key so I could let myself in and wait for him.

I know I said I was against doing that, but I'd missed him so much when he was away ... we managed to steal a moment in the kitchen for a kiss this morning and I was burning up in his arms. He said all the time he'd been lying in his hotel room, he'd been thinking about me ... It's just impossible for us to keep our hands off each other. I couldn't say no.

I waited ages at the flat, but Dan didn't show. Then Scott, the bloke who owns the place, turned up. He was about as leery as that flippin' Essex boy, all 'wink, wink, nudge, nudge'. He went, 'Oh, sorry, thought you'd be finished by now', which made me go really red. When I said Dan had been held up, he said, 'Suppose that's the name of the game, isn't it?' It was so embarrassing, I couldn't stand it any longer, and I shot off feeling like some cheap little scrubber. I passed Grant Mitchell on my way home from Walford Tube Station and I remembered screaming at him in the Vic for being an adulterer. Who am I to talk? Look at me. Bianca Butcher, married with a kid, having it off with her mother's fiancé. I thought Grant and Louise were the lowest forms of life on the planet, but until today I couldn't admit to myself that I'd joined them. I disgust myself.

I got in to find Mum and Dan having a blazing row about something – turned out he'd forgotten all about Billy's custody hearing until she phoned up from the court and reminded him. He got there really late – too late to be of any help – which was why he didn't show at the flat. That's when it really hit home. Billy's whole future was on the line today and we were sneaking round trying to find half-an-hour for a grope. It's pathetic. At least it brought me to my senses, though. I decided there and then that we couldn't carry on like this. I told Dan I was gonna go and stay in Manchester for a few days, do my interview, have a look around and sort my head out. Dan wasn't that happy about it, but like I told him, one of us has got to be strong, and if he can't get his act together, I'm gonna have to. For everyone's sake.

Ricky was even more hacked off than Dan when I told him my plan. He doesn't want me to go to college, he wants to us to live in a Barrett Home and sprog. He said he was the one trying to plan for our future, and that was when I really lost my rag with him. I said, 'That's just it. I don't want my future planned for me. And I certainly don't want it to be about work benches and garden swings.'

He said, 'There's nothing wrong with that stuff. It's what people do,' and I said, 'Well it's not what I want to do. I want more than that.' Ricky stormed out and left me sitting in the living room all by myself. I felt so low, I just broke down in tears. It was like this was the beginning of the end, not just for me and Ricky, but for me and Dan. I have never felt more alone in my entire life.

20 August

I'm in Manchester. Had my interview today – total disaster. I made such an idiot of myself. They must have thought I had a screw loose. The thing is, it was going really well until they started asking me all these questions about my private life. I'd had a look round and really liked what I saw. I mean, it was a bit scary at first, all these departments, but dead exciting. You do a foundation course in stuff like ceramics, sculpture, fine art, 3-D and interior design, and then I could specialize in fashion design in my third year. It was a million miles away from flogging clothes in Bridge Street Market, but I somehow felt I could fit in. And they had this brilliant crêche, too … bright and sunny and full of toys, Liam would love it. The girl who showed me round said that the college was pro students with kids, cos they're more responsible. That was when I thought, yeah, I could do this…

Then I had my interview and the panel seemed to like my portfolio (bit of a rush job – I spent the whole of last weekend doing sketches of designs!). They asked me what themes influenced my work and I said oriental, cos I love Japanese kimono shapes and embroidery. They asked me who my favourite designer was, and I said Vivienne Westwood and Alexander McQueen. It sounds weird to say this about an interview, but I was really enjoying myself. It was so good to talk about fashion. I don't get the chance to do that normally – I mean, I read magazines, keep up with the collections, what's new, what's coming up, etc., and of course I talk to the wholesalers, but this was something else. This was people taking an interest in what I thought, and it was great.

The woman who was asking most of the questions, Alison Wylie, was the head of the fashion and textiles department. She asked me where I saw myself in ten years' time and I said I'd like to have my own design company, see Madonna at some big awards wearing one of my dresses. But I said I also wanted to design for chain stores, cos that's one of the things I love about running the stall – seeing ordinary people buy something they can afford that's going to make them look good. I mean, everyone's got a right to look their best. Mrs Wylie said I had a 'very commendable attitude', which sounded like I was doing alright.

Then she started asking me personal questions, and I just fell apart. I'd done all the preparation for the fashion stuff, but when they said, 'How would it affect your family life?' I couldn't answer. I started thinking, how does Liam fit into this, and Ricky? She asked if Ricky was OK about moving up to Manchester and all I could say was, 'I don't know'. I tried to explain things, but I got more and more muddled and in the end I said, 'I'm sorry, I think I'd better go', and rushed off in tears. It was like, I'd found something for me at long last, but there were so many things in the way. I don't know what's happening with my marriage, with Dan ... I don't even know who I am any more.

I went back to my hotel room feeling a total failure. I was thinking about packing my stuff and heading home right then, when there was a knock and this voice said, 'Room service, special delivery'. I opened the door and there was Dan, clutching a bottle of Champagne. I was so relieved to see him, I just fell into his arms, crying my eyes out. He said he'd made up some excuse to Mum about going to a trade fair, because he had to see me. All my resolve about being strong crumbled in about ten seconds flat. I know it's wrong, but when he kisses me, I just melt. And I felt so vulnerable and needed to be held so badly...

21 August

It was wonderful to wake up with Dan. That's what I've been dying to do for ages, wake up with his arms wrapped around me, feel him snuggled up close and make love, all drowsy and sexy and slow. It was even better than what I'd dreamt it would be!

We spent all morning walking round Manchester hand-in-hand and kissing like a couple of love-struck kids. It was so good to be able to show our feelings for each other and not to have to sneak around. Dan took me on a canal cruise and we drank Champagne and watched the world go by. It was as if none of our other hassles existed, like we'd taken time out from our real lives. I discovered he'd found those old photos of me and him that I'd put in my bag, and we talked about how things used to be between us. I said I used to think it was great, going out with a bloke from the rag trade, because I've always loved clothes. In a way, meeting Dan when I was fifteen was what sparked my interest in fashion.

Dan had booked us into this swish four-star hotel, and we spent the whole afternoon together in bed. I felt really guilty afterwards, but Dan said he had a foolproof method of dealing with guilt, and went and emptied the minibar of chocolate! So now I know how he copes! I wanted to spend the night there so badly, but I knew I had to get back to my grotty guesthouse, in case Ricky called. Dan came over later, despite me telling him to wait 'til I'd phoned him, bringing with him more Champagne ... and more chocolate. I tried to be stern, but it was impossible. How can a girl resist such a man?

I was on cloud nine when I got up this morning. That's cos I thought Dan was as deeply in love with me as I am with him. How wrong can you be, eh? I should've learned by now, shouldn't I? When a bloke says he loves you, it's only while he's doing the business. Mention the 'L' word out of bed and they run a mile. Only, I thought Dan was different. I thought he really meant it. Now, I don't know any more.

Last night Dan held me and told me I was incredible and he couldn't think of anything but me. This morning he told me I'd got too serious. I couldn't believe my ears. I said, 'I suppose you just wanted a bit on the side, no strings attached', and he went, 'Yes, and so did you. It was meant to be passionate, not painful'. It took my breath away. He pursued me all the way up here and for the past two days he's done nothing but tell me he loves me. Suddenly I'm just a fling, a sordid little affair that's got to be kept secret.

Dan expects me to go home and carry on like nothing's happened, but I can't. I told him that and he got angry and said, 'You'll have to'. But it ain't that simple. He's taken over my life. He's changed me. I'm not the Bianca I knew, I'm someone else … someone on the edge of a new life. And I need Dan in it.

We left Manchester after breakfast and got on the motorway, stopping at a service station for lunch. I couldn't eat anything, though, I was too churned up. I said, 'This is stupid, we've got to decide what to do, it's driving me mad.' Dan went ballistic. He said I'd ruin everything if I came clean and the only option was to live a lie. I said there was another option – tell the truth, leave Walford and live together in Manchester – but he said that could never happen because he couldn't leave Mum.

Guess how big I felt after that? In a two-horse race with my mum, I lose. What's she got, that I ain't? Apart from wrinkles and stretch-marks from having four kids? Dan said, 'I do love you, but Carol needs me more than you.' So what, he's a charity now, is he? I was so hurt, I walked off in tears, but there was nowhere to go except the car park and we was stuck in the middle of the M6, so I had to get back into the car.

That wasn't the final insult, though. Dan stopped the car at a station miles out of London and told me to get the train the rest of the way home. He tried to twist my words, saying I was the one worried about being seen together and we shouldn't arrive back at the same time, but I knew he wanted to get shot of me. He even had the nerve to offer me money, like I was some cheap tart he'd paid for the weekend. I stood on the platform and watched him drive off, with tears streaming down my face. If he didn't break my heart properly last time, he's finished the job now.

23 August

Today I got one of the things I wanted most in the world, and lost the other.

The good thing is, the college has offered me a place. I couldn't believe it when Ricky brought the letter round to the stall. I thought I didn't stand a chance after the way I cocked up my interview, but the letter said they were very impressed with me and they wanted me to start in September. Ricky was really negative about it, moaning about how it was gonna turn our lives upside down, but it wasn't really his reaction I was bothered about, it was Dan's.

Dan's reaction was to dump me. He didn't actually know I'd got in at Manchester, I just asked him what would happen between us if I did. He said it would be a clean break, and when I told him I couldn't turn my feelings off like that, he said this was getting too heavy and he was ending it. He changed his tune though, after Mum came over and spilled the beans. Once Dan found out I was leaving in a few weeks, he was all over me again, wanting to carry on 'til I go. He said it made sense now!!! I thought, oh, yeah, that would be a good deal for

Dan, keep his bit on the side while it suits him, then get married to Mum and live happily ever after.

So I called his bluff. I told him I was gonna stay. Dan said, 'You can't just throw it all away', but I said, 'I've already thrown away my marriage and my family. Do you think I did that for a laugh?' He went, 'You stay and we're finished anyway,' in a nasty voice. I wasn't gonna be walked all over like that, so I said, 'We'll see about that. I'm not fifteen any more. It's over when I say so and not 'til then.' I felt so used. Not just sexually, but emotionally. I've put everything on the line for Dan and suddenly I'm nothing more than a bad habit to him. He ain't gonna get away with treating me like that, not this time. I'm gonna stay and be a thorn in his side and make him regret what he's done every single day of his life.

It's so hard, keeping all this to myself. Writing it down helps, but I've been desperate to talk to someone about it. Nat knows my history with Dan, but I ain't told her the rest … as it is, she keeps nagging me to tell Ricky the truth. I wish Tiff was here. She'd have listened. And she wouldn't have judged. If Tiff was around, I wouldn't have ended up blurting it all out to Pat, which was what I did this evening. Pat found me in the kiddies' playground, blubbing on one of the swings, and asked me what was wrong. She soon sussed I wasn't being straight with her, and made me tell her the whole story. So I did.

Pat was horrified, of course. Said I couldn't have done more damage if I'd tried. Then she said I had no choice but to end it with Dan, go to Manchester with Ricky and forget the whole thing ever happened. I told her that's what Dan wanted, but I wasn't gonna let him get away with it. There's only one thing that stands out clearly in all this mess, and that is that Mum and Ricky deserve to hear the truth. Nat's right, besides I'm fed up with lying. And what's the point, if Dan doesn't want me? I might as well burn my boats good and proper. I always said Mum should know what a bastard she's marrying. As for poor old Ricky, he already knows I'm a bitch. He just don't know how much of a one. It's time he found out.

24 August

Mum's pregnant. I just can't believe it. I've been working myself up to telling her and Ricky all day, but Ricky disappeared off somewhere and when I finally got a chance to sit down with Mum, she dropped this little bombshell. She's eight weeks gone and sitting there telling me how right this baby feels, and all the time I'm thinking about what Dan and me were doing when she was already pregnant. I said, 'Maybe you should ask Dan what he thinks about all this,' and she went, 'I have and he wants this baby more than anything'. Just then, Dan appeared in the kitchen. He didn't say anything, just walked over to Mum and put his hand on her shoulder and stared at me, as if to say, so what are you gonna do now? I was too choked to speak and ran upstairs. I've been crying on the bed ever since. I always knew Dan was a two-timing, cheating rat but I never thought even he was capable of this. But how can I possibly tell Mum now? This makes it impossible...

25 August

Got no sleep last night. I feel like the living dead, and look like it too, judging by the remarks I've had from the other stall-holders. I just can't get my head round what Mum told me yesterday. How could she let this happen? I mean, she's got four children by four different men, you'd've thought she'd have learnt by now. I mean, I got enough lectures about taking precautions. What's she trying to do? Replace Billy? She's given up on getting custody of him, perhaps that's it. Or was she trying to trick Dan into marrying her? Putting a ring on his finger won't keep him faithful. Cheating's in Dan's nature. He's proved that with me. And where will she be? A single mum of forty with five kids. That must be some kind of record.

As for that slimeball ... I saw Dan this morning and he insisted Mum didn't tell him about the baby until he got back from Manchester. I said, 'And that makes everything all right, does it?' I mean, a couple of days ago, Dan was all for us carrying on until I went to college, and he sure as hell knew then. He says he feels guilty and comes out with this guff about facing up to his responsibilities, but I don't think he knows the meaning of the word. I thought Dan was sincere, but I'm seeing him in a whole new light these days. He's a chancer, out for whatever he can get away with, no matter who he hurts.

Ricky came home early this evening, much to my relief. We'd had a row about Manchester and he went off yesterday without saying where he was going. He didn't come home all night and I was getting really worried. I thought perhaps he'd sussed about me and Dan, especially when he said he'd been up to Manchester, but it turned out he was trying to make a new start for us. Frank's lined him up a job as a trainee manager at his car business up there, and Ricky's found us somewhere to live with a garden for Liam. He's even checked out the bus route to college for me.

I was so touched, I could feel myself welling up. I'd been determined to tell Ricky about me and Dan, but he was so enthusiastic and he'd got everything sorted and when I got the chance, I just couldn't. The words were on the tip of my tongue, but then Ricky said something that stopped me. He said, 'I love you, B. I might not have shown that much lately, but this is what it's all about. Not many people get a second chance. If I thought I'd blown it with you, I don't know what I'd do.'

It made me realize what a wonderful bloke Ricky is. He's not the one who should be begging for a second chance, it's me. I don't deserve it, but there he was, offering it to me – to all of us – on a plate. He said, 'We can make it work. There's nothing to stop us trying, is there?', and I thought, he's right.

Maybe we can save something. Maybe this could all work out, after all. And so I agreed.

30 August

It's a relief to have made up my mind, at last. Pat was right, what she said the other day. If I told everyone, I'd only end up hurting them. It'd have destroyed the entire family, and I can't do that, just cos I'm on some crusade to tell the truth. Mum don't deserve a rat like Dan, but there's nothing I can do about it. And maybe he will buckle down, who knows? Fatherhood might be just what he needs. He failed at it in his first marriage, but that might make him really commit himself this time round. That's what he keeps telling me, anyway.

The best thing for everyone is for me to get clean away from Walford. At least then I'm the only one who gets hurt. I can handle that. I should suffer for what I've done. But Mum, the baby, Ricky, Liam, they're all innocents in this situation. If I keep my mouth shut, it lets Dan off the hook, but I can't make other people pay the price for our mess. Anyway, if I'm really honest, the main reason I wanted the truth to come out was to get revenge on Dan. Well, I've made up my mind. He ain't worth it.

Ricky and me told the family about Manchester at breakfast this morning. They was all a bit surprised, cos I'd said we were staying here, but I told them Ricky being offered this job had changed everything. We're going at the end of this week – term starts soon – and there's loads to sort out before then. Of course, Dan was all for it, but Sonia got really upset and went running out the room in tears.

Mum and I had a little chat at the caff later. She asked if I was going cos I was angry about the baby. I told her no, I was doing this for me, which ain't the whole truth but it'll do. I know she's really proud, cos I'm the first Jackson to go to college. She told me she envied me, cos I was doing something with my life. If she knew the real reason, she wouldn't think I was so great, she'd hate my guts.

Things are still a bit delicate between me and Ricky, but we're both making an effort. Natalie suggested we come to the reopening of E20, now that Beppe's running it (Steve's in prison, awaiting trial, along with Matthew). I wasn't that keen at first, but it seemed like a good way for me and Ricky to spend some time together, and we need to build bridges. It was hard to get into the swing of things, at first, but then we had a dance and Ricky started larking around and I began to relax. I might even have enjoyed myself if Mum and Dan hadn't decided to come along on the spur of the moment. That was my cue to go.

I don't want to be in the same room as Dan. Despite everything he's said, he still stares at me, still tries to get me on my own. Even this evening, before we came out, he asked me if Manchester was really what I wanted. I said, 'What do you care? The only important thing now is that you and me get as far away from each other as possible.' He gave me that look that used to make my knees melt, but luckily Ricky barged in at that point. I can't wait for the next few days to pass and we can be off. I feel as if I'm sitting on a timebomb.

31 August

Spent the day packing up. We've got so much gear, I can't believe it. Having a baby doubles your stuff overnight. I gave all Liam's newborn clothes to Mum. She was well chuffed. We ended up going through a box of baby things that used to belong to me and Robbie and having a laugh together. I asked which was the best bit for her, and Mum said when we was tiny and couldn't answer back! I can tell she's really looking forward to this baby – she's nesting already.

Dan came in and spoiled the moment and I had to get out of the house. I said I had a headache and went to the Square gardens, but Mum knew it was an excuse, cos she sent Dan out to see what the matter was. This time, amazingly, we managed to have a half-civilized conversation – well, to start with. I told him I'd got a whole new life ahead of me and he started to get sentimental, saying he wished things had been different. I said, 'You can't live in the past, it's dead,' and he went, 'Are you absolutely sure about that?' Talk about not knowing when to stop. I told him to tear up the old photo of us I'd given him, cos I'd torn up mine, and I think that really hurt him. He said I was fooling myself if I thought I could be happy with Ricky after what we'd had together. I said, 'It's what I want.'

And it is, now. There's no point in dwelling on what might have been. I'm lucky I've still got a husband who loves me. That's enough. It ain't a grand passion, but we are friends, and that counts for a lot. OK, so I'm not head over heels in love with Ricky like I was with Dan, but that kind of love is too destructive. Better to be mates who are there for each other. The rest I can live without. I've had that side of me awakened, and look what it did ... turned me into a selfish, lying, cheating bitch. Sex ain't everything. It's loyalty that really counts.

2 September

Everyone knows. My life is in ruins. Mum's disowned me, Ricky don't ever want to see me again and Robbie and Sonia won't talk to me neither. I'm at Pat and Roy's now. Pat weren't too keen on taking me in, but Mum threw me and Liam out into the night and I had nowhere else to go. If it weren't for Liam, I don't know what I'd do. I'm that desperate...

It's my fault Mum found out. Dan was coming on to me earlier in the day, telling me he still loved me and all that crap. He showed me the photo I'd given him and said he couldn't bring himself to destroy it cos we still had something special. It was like twisting a knife in my guts. I told him we'd got nothing and snatched the photo off him, ripped it up and threw it in the bin. I never thought anyone would find it and put the pieces together, but that's exactly what Mum did.

It happened while me and Ricky was over at the Vic, celebrating Mel and Ian's engagement and saying our goodbyes to everyone. We was happy, though it's hard to believe that now. We were dancing and kissing and he told me how much he loved me. I'd been playing Cupid with Nat and Barry, and got him to propose to her at last, and me and Nat was having a little conflab about it in the Ladies when Mum walked in. She said she wanted to speak to me, so Nat made herself scarce. Then Mum said, 'I've just had a long chat to Dan. About this,' and she dropped the bits of photo on the counter.

I was so shocked I couldn't speak. She said, 'He's told me everything,' and my heart sank like a stone. I said, 'I'm so sorry, I didn't want to hurt you,' and she said I should have talked to her and it would have been OK if I'd just come clean. I couldn't believe she was taking it so well. I was blurting out apologies, trying to explain, and I'd dug myself in too deep before I realized that Mum didn't know the whole story, she only knew that me and Dan had a past. She went storming out into the bar and when I tried to talk to her, she screamed at me in front of the whole pub, calling me a dirty lying little slag. Then she slapped me. I could hear the sound of it ringing in the silence. The place was packed and everyone was staring at me. Mum went out and nobody moved and I thought the moment would never end. Then I realized Ricky weren't there and I knew I had to get to him before she did.

When I got to the house, Mum and Dan were rowing and Ricky was looking all bemused, asking what was going on. Mum saw me and said, 'Go on, tell him, cos if you don't, I will,' and I knew she meant it. She had this wild look in her eyes and she grabbed hold of me and shoved me towards Ricky. I didn't have a choice. After all the times I'd rehearsed breaking it to him gently, it just came out, the blunt, ugly truth.

I said, 'I've been sleeping with Dan.' Ricky didn't believe me at first, he thought it was a wind-up. I was crying and repeating, 'I'm sorry, I'm so sorry'. I told him Dan meant nothing to me and Ricky looked at me in total disgust, like I was dog shit on his shoe, and said, 'Yeah, well I know how he feels'. Then he walked out.

Liam was crying and I fled upstairs to be with him. I was shaking and sobbing, raining tears down on him as I leaned over his cot, and it just made my poor baby cry even harder. I could hear all this crashing and screaming from downstairs – it sounded as if Mum was smashing the place up. Then the door slammed and it went quiet. I half-expected her to come up and physically attack me, the state she was in. I sat on the bed, clutching Liam, rocking backwards and forwards like I used to when I was a kid. It was ages before I could get a grip, and even longer before I could get Liam to settle again.

I hardly dared go back downstairs, but I knew I had to face the music. I found Mum in the living-room, slumped in a chair. I said I didn't want a row, I just wanted to explain, but she wouldn't listen. She said we was finished. I said, 'But I'm your daughter, you can't hate me forever', and she went, 'You're not my daughter. My daughter's a sweet little five-year-old worried about having freckles and the wrong colour hair. You're just some selfish slag. I don't even know you.'

As far as she was concerned, I was the Other Woman who had stolen her bloke. No matter how I explained that I'd tried to stop it and I didn't do it to hurt her, she thought I'd gone after Dan deliberately to wreck her happiness. I told her it wasn't like that, that I loved Dan and it had all spun out of control, but she said that was all lies and excuses.

Even when I told her it was over and I'd realized my future was with Ricky, she didn't let up. She said I was selfish and I always had been, just like David, and then she started harping on the same old record, blaming me for everything that had gone wrong in her life and all the chances she'd missed to bring me up. As if I ain't heard that one a million times! I started to get angry then and told her a few home-truths. I mean, she ain't so bloody perfect. She slept with David behind Alan's back. She can call it 'unfinished business' if she likes, but then so was me and Dan. And anyway, if I'd had a different childhood, I might not have grown up so insecure that I needed to throw myself at a married man when I was just fifteen.

Mum said, 'Nice try, Bianca, but you ain't gonna get through to me. Nothing you can say will make up for what you've done.' She said at least I could move on, whereas she was stuck with a baby again. That was when I saw my chance – how I could make it up to her. I told her I was gonna stay and support her, but she knocked me back and said it was over. 'I can't even bear to look at you', those were her words. She said I'd always remind her of Dan, just like the baby would.

It was awful. She wouldn't listen to a word. I had one last go, trying to explain that I'd stopped it as soon as I knew about the baby and she went, 'Poor Bianca, your torrid little affair, cut off in its prime'. I said, 'Mum, please, it weren't what you think. I never stopped feeling terrible, thinking about you.' I told her it had only happened twice and it was never planned, that the last time he'd just turned up in Manchester out of the blue. She turned deathly pale and slumped forward with her head in her hands. I asked what the matter was and she said, 'He already knew. I told him I was pregnant the day before'. I felt totally sickened. I couldn't believe Dan could have been so heartless, so manipulative. I said, 'Mum, I had no idea', and she told me to go. She couldn't bear any more, just threw me and Liam out into the night. And that's when I ran into Dan.

If I hadn't seen him for what he was before, I certainly did then. He was just looking for a get-out, some lie that would get him off the hook with Mum. His attitude disgusted me. 'Another day and we'd have been in the clear', that's what he said. I told him he revolted me and said that I knew everything about him now. He went, 'Meaning what?' and I told him what Mum had said about the baby. Even then, he tried to wriggle out of it, and then he had the nerve to put it on me, saying he'd come up to break it off but it had 'gone off the rails' when he found me in tears. I said I could see straight through him now, that it was one lie to cover up another with him. Dan knew if he'd told me Mum was pregnant, I'd have been straight out the door. I went, 'You see, we're different, you and me. Beyond a certain point I will not go.' Know what he said? 'I made a mistake, that's all.' Understatement of the decade. Dan can't even see what he's done wrong. He still thinks him and Mum can get back together. I told him, he's lost me and he's lost her, and if he tried to hurt Mum again I'd kill him.

Pat took me in – mainly because of Liam, I think. I was carrying him wrapped up in a blanket like a little refugee. I left him with her and went over the Vic to find Ricky, but he wasn't there. It was so humiliating. Everyone was pointing and whispering, and Peggy called me a vamp and told me to get out, and even Frank, who's usually on my side, turned his back on me. Worst of all was seeing the look on Robbie's and Sonia's faces. They wouldn't even talk to me.

I went to the Arches, cos that was the only other place Ricky could be, and found him there, drinking. I begged him to listen to me, told him I'd do anything, tell him anything to keep him. He said, 'Anything but the truth', and I said, 'No, I'll tell you the truth, I swear it, just give me one more chance.' He made me tell him all the sordid details – when me and Dan kissed, where we'd made love, how many times. He kept on and on interrogating me – was it good, was I satisfied? It made me feel sick just talking about it. I told him the sex wasn't important, it would have worn off, and he went, 'Like it did for us?'

He was so hurt and so bitter, and everything I said just made things worse and worse. I couldn't think straight, I was so tired and upset and he was firing these questions at me. It must've sounded terrible to him. It sounded bad enough from where I was standing. I let slip about Dan being with me in Manchester and as soon as the words were out of my mouth, I could see Ricky was totally devastated. I couldn't look him in the eye, but he grabbed hold of me and forced me to look at him. He said, 'You were just using me, weren't you? Free babysitting and someone cosy to come home to. That's all I've ever been and you would have dragged me up to Manchester, made me give up everything to tide you over.' I said it wasn't like that and I still wanted to go with him, but he pushed me away. He called me a selfish little slut and said he didn't want anything more to do with me.

I was pleading with him and trying to cling on to him, but he shoved me really hard and I went flying and hit my head against a car. Ricky just stared at me like I was someone else, someone he didn't know or even care about. My head was spinning, but I managed to crawl on to my knees. I thought he was gonna help me up but instead he turned and walked away.

I don't know how long I sat there in the cold and the dirt and the oil. I didn't have the strength to get up. I kept thinking of when Tiff fell down the stairs and hit her head. I was waiting for something to happen. I thought, I could collapse and die and no-one would know. Ricky didn't come back. No-one came looking for me. There wasn't a person left in Albert Square who cared whether I lived or died.

6 September

Ricky won't see me. I asked Pat to go over the Vic for me – I didn't dare go in – but he won't have anything to do with me. Mum won't talk to me neither. She's even had the locks changed. I saw Sonia, but she just froze me out, told me I wasn't welcome there no more. I felt like the lowest of the low. People were gassing about me in the street. I could see them, staring at me through the windows of the shop and the caff, all getting off on the gossip, 'Bianca Butcher, Fallen Woman', or summat like that. Don't they just love it. It's like rubber-neckers at a car accident. The Jacksons have had a smash-up, come and have a gawp. They're sick, the whole lot of them.

I tried Ricky again later, at the Arches. He kept ignoring me until I said, 'What about Liam? I know you hate me, but do you hate him, too?' I mean, Liam ain't done nothing wrong, he still deserves to see his dad. Ricky got really angry. He was shouting at me not to use Liam to get to him. He said, 'He's my son and he always will be. What I've got with him is nothing to do with you. It won't change just because his Mum's a tart.'

I just wandered round in a daze after that. I didn't know what to do. I ain't got a home and I don't know what's gonna happen to me and Liam. I don't even know what I'm gonna do in the next five minutes, let alone tomorrow or the next day. I sat in the Square gardens, watching the house, hoping Mum would come out and I could talk to her, but her bedroom curtains stayed closed and there was no sign of her. I dunno how long I sat there – seemed like hours. I was cuddling Liam and Pat came and took him off me in the end, but I still couldn't bring myself to go in.

Then I saw Dan heading towards me and I panicked. I yelled, 'Stay away from me', but he grabbed hold of my arm and pulled me close. I said, 'How can you live with yourself? I can't.' The look on his face took me by surprise. He was haggard and grey and close to tears. He said, 'I know, it's been hell', and I said, 'That's where we belong.' He was almost leaning on my shoulder, his head bowed. He said, 'I tried to fight it, but I couldn't help it. I wanted you so much.' I told him it was too late for that now and I wished I'd never laid eyes on him, I'd been happy with Ricky. He said, 'No you weren't. We couldn't get enough of each other and you know it.'

In my heart of hearts I knew that was true, but I wasn't gonna admit it to him. What I did was wrong, but what Dan did was worse. I was so madly in love with him, I couldn't see the wood for the trees, but Dan knew what he was doing. He manipulated me, he set up our meetings, he organized his mate's flat that time and tricked me into going, he turned up uninvited when I went to Manchester. Yeah, I was stupid to go along with it, but I resisted as much as I could. Dan made all the running and when things got too hot for him to handle, he was the one abusing Mum's and my trust. And our love. She and I have both been betrayed, but it's harder for her, she thought Dan was Mr Wonderful. I always knew he was a lying, cheating scumbag, I just chose to forget about it, but she thought the sun shone out of his backside. I said to Dan, 'In a way, I'm glad Mum found out about us. At least now she knows you for what you are. I feel sorry for that baby.' I mean, what kind of a life has that little one got to look forward to?

7 September

I keep thinking things are so bad they can't possibly get any worse, and then they do. Ricky wants to divorce me and get custody of Liam. I found out this morning. I had plucked up courage and called round to the Vic in the hopes of persuading Ricky to talk to me, but he said he was off to see Marcus Christie and the question of custody was top of his list. I said, 'We're a family, he needs us both,' but he wouldn't listen, even when I told him I'd written to the college, cancelling my course. I don't know what to do. He can't take my baby away, he can't. Liam's all I've got. He's my flesh and blood. He's my every-thing. If I ain't got Liam, my life wouldn't be worth living. Ricky might as well kill me, cos that's what it would do to me.

I suppose I imagined every woman felt that way about her child. That's why I didn't believe Dan at first when he burst in to Pat's and said he thought Mum was gonna get rid of her baby. He was in a real state. He said she'd threatened it the other night and now she'd gone off in a taxi without saying where. I ran round to the house and asked Sonia, but she was in the dark, too. She said that Mum had been acting 'a bit weird' and ripped a page out of the phone book before rushing off. I found the phone book and my stomach turned over. The missing page was from the section on abortion clinics. I phoned the cab firm Mum had used – there was a card by the phone – and they confirmed the rest.

I didn't tell Dan. It'd make things a thousand times worse if Mum saw him. I had to go and talk her out of it, and if Dan came, she'd freak. I know Mum, she'd dig her heels in and do the opposite to what Dan wanted, just to get back at him. Anyway, he's got no place in her life and the further away he stays from her the better. Dan was waiting for me outside the house – Sonia wouldn't let him in – and I played it cool and fed him some excuse about Mum going for a hospital check-up. He weren't entirely convinced, but I managed to shake him off.

When I got to the clinic, the receptionist wouldn't help me. She said it was clinic policy not to reveal clients' names. I waited until her back was turned, then legged it through some swing doors and into the waiting area. And there was Mum. I could tell she was shocked to see me. Then her face hardened and I knew I was in for a battle. She got up and walked off down the corridor without saying anything and beckoned me into a side room. Her eyes were blazing. She said, 'What the hell are you doing here?' I told her she wasn't in a fit state to make a decision like this, but she wouldn't wear it. She said it was her baby and she didn't want it, end of story.

I said, 'This is a baby we're talking about. You can't just get rid of it cos you're angry,' but she wouldn't listen. She said the baby would remind her of Dan every day of her life and she couldn't cope with that. I told her the baby wasn't Dan, it was a separate person, but she wouldn't budge. I said, 'It's like saying you wished you'd got rid of Robbie or Sonia,' and she went, 'Or you. Yeah, I'd settle for you.'

My own mother hates me so much she wishes I'd never been born. I was so choked, I could hardly speak. My father paid to have me aborted. And now my mother wishes she'd done it. She told me she went down the clinic when she was fifteen, but couldn't go through with it. The bitterness was pouring out of her – how she'd signed her life away for me and I wasn't worth it, how she wished she could get shot of me, just like this baby.

I was fighting for the baby's life, but nothing seemed to be getting through. I said, 'Are you telling me you ain't got any feelings for it? Nothing at all?', and then she admitted she had. She said part of her was crying out to have it, but she wasn't gonna do it. She wanted to get rid of all traces of Dan, get him out of her head. 'I just want some peace, Bianca', those were her words. I could see she was crumbling then. I said, 'And you think you'll get it doing this? Well you won't and you know it.'

She started to cry and I put my arms around her. I told her it was gonna be all right, I'd take care of her and the baby. She sobbed like a child, and I could feel the poison draining out of her and I knew then it would be OK. Only I was wrong. Just as I was leading her out of the clinic, Mum stopped and said she wasn't coming. She had got herself together by then and was quite calm. She said, 'I'm not doing this to hurt you, Bianca, or to hurt Dan.' I tried to persuade her to go home, sleep on it, but she'd made up her mind. I could fight her rage, but not this quiet, calm determination. She said she'd spent her entire life crashing from one disaster to another, taking what happened, and this time she wasn't gonna do that. There was nothing I could say to bring her round. She wouldn't even let me stay.

I walked out through the swing doors into the night. It was getting dark and there was a chill in the air, the first hint of autumn. As I went down the clinic steps, the truth hit me like the rush of cold air on my face. It was all my fault. I'd killed that baby. Because of my stupidness and selfishness, a little life was gonna be taken away. My own half-sister or brother. No matter what Mum said now, a few days ago she was over the moon about having it. She didn't see the baby as ruining her life, she saw it as a chance for a new one.

The thought overwhelmed me. Suddenly, my legs felt so weak I could hardly stand. I slumped down on the steps, my head in my hands, my shoulders jerking with sobs. A woman stopped and asked if I was all right, but I couldn't speak, just shook my head and cried and cried. It had been so painful, being in that clinic, reminding me of the time I'd thought about aborting Natasha. I'd gone to a clinic, too. I nearly went through with it, like Mum nearly aborted me, but I didn't in the end. And I was so, so glad. Then we found out all the things that was wrong with her and it changed everything. I had a termination at twenty weeks and it was the hardest thing I'd ever done. But Natasha wouldn't have had a life worth living. This baby did.

I always thought that losing Natasha was some sort of punishment for considering an abortion in the first place. So what's this? My punishment for doing what I did with Dan? Mum said she didn't want to hurt me, but she's wrenched something out of me tonight that I don't know whether I'll ever be able to get back. My self-respect. I hate myself more than I can say. I've always been so quick to judge other people, to accuse, tear a strip off them. And I never once looked at myself. Grant taunted me in the street today. He said, 'Not so high and mighty now, are you? Ends up, we're just the same.' I told him I wasn't some pig who killed his wife, but look what I've done! I've murdered a baby! I'm not the same as Grant Mitchell, I'm worse. I don't know how I'm ever gonna be able to live with that.

Ricky came round this morning. He's started divorce proceedings but he's not going after custody of Liam, thank God. I held my baby close and he peeped up at me with bright trusting eyes and I felt like howling. He's got no idea what a terrible thing his mummy's done. I feel so guilty, it's eating me up. I told Ricky about Mum having an abortion and how awful I felt, and I could see it touched him, too. He wanted to comfort me, I know he did. I begged him to give me another chance, a chance for us to be a family again with Liam, and for a few seconds he looked as if he was gonna come round. Then the doorbell rang and when I went to get it, there was Dan. He was demanding to know what had happened with Mum and wouldn't be put off, so I told him to meet me in George Street later. When I got back to the kitchen, Ricky had gone. He must've overheard me. I couldn't believe my bad luck.

I was trying to get him on the phone, to explain, when the doorbell rang again. This time it was Barry and Natalie, wanting to talk wedding arrangements with Pat. Barry was going on about wanting a big do, and Natalie looked at me coldly and said, 'Was yours a day to remember?' I said it was, and she went, 'That's nice. D'you have all the normal vows? Or did you miss a few out?' I was stunned. Nat's never spoken to me like that before. After all we've been through, I thought she of all people would understand. I said, 'You're meant to be my friend', and she said, 'I am your friend. I'm your only friend. That's how sad you are.'

After they'd gone, I didn't know what to do with myself. I knew I ought to go and meet Dan, but I was totally dreading it. I did start out to see him, but then I saw Sonia crying outside the caff and Robbie comforting her, and I knew I had to go and explain. Sonia said, 'How can you live with yourself? If I was you I'd just want to curl up and die.' I told them I'd tried to stop Mum, but Sonia said she didn't even want to look at me and Robbie threw me out of the caff. I couldn't face Dan's anger after that. I knew he'd explode, blame me, and I was worried what he'd do to Mum when he found out the truth.

I went back to Pat's and kept my head down, but Dan barged in through the back door, demanding to know what had happened. He was really hacked off and said he could tell from my face I was lying about Mum going for a hospital check-up. He said, 'Tell me or I'll go over there now and drag it out of her.' I could see he meant it, so I bought time by telling him Mum had gone to the clinic, but that I'd stopped her from going through with the abortion. All the anger seemed to go out of him and he looked all vulnerable and said, 'But the baby's OK?' What could I do? I said yes. I know it was a stupid thing to do, but I really thought he'd stay away from her if I asked him to give her some space.

When I went out to the postbox later, Dan came flying up behind me and grabbed me. He shook me and started ranting, 'You conniving little bitch, you put her up to this, didn't you? She's murdered my kid. Do you know what that feels like, do you have any idea?' He was going mad – his face was all red and he was snarling and spitting and shouting in my face. I was really scared. I cried, 'What have you done to her?' but he ignored me and went, 'Well, let's see how you like it.'

Next thing I knew, he'd scooped Liam out of his pram and was holding him high in the air, above his head, like he was gonna smash him on the ground. I screamed for help but he was taunting me and going, 'Scared? Do you understand? I want you to understand what this feels like'. Liam was wailing and kicking and my heart was in my mouth. I was so terrified Dan would drop him. Robbie saw and came over and I told him to run and get Ricky. I was pleading, 'Please, Dan, Liam ain't done anything wrong', trying to get through to him. I'd never seen him like that. He'd lost it completely. I was so frightened. Liam was struggling and I thought he was gonna slip out of his coat and fall ... Dan went, 'I really wanted that child. Now it's gone, like that, a whole life...' I could feel hysteria building up inside me, but I knew I had to stay calm and reason with him. I put my hand on Dan's arm and said, 'I know. I've lost a kid, too. But hurting Liam ain't gonna help, is it?' My touch seemed to connect with him and he looked around, stunned, as if he'd just become aware of what he was doing. He lowered Liam down and handed him to me and I clutched my baby tight. When I looked up from soothing him, Dan was walking away towards the Vic.

Just as I was settling Liam back into his pram, Ricky came panting round the corner, frantic. I told him about Dan and said that Liam was OK, but Ricky was furious with me for putting Liam at risk. I said it wasn't my fault, but he said it was, and that it was just gonna go on getting worse and worse until I cleared out of Walford. His parting words were, 'We don't want you here, none of us. Just go away'. The hatred in his eyes almost floored me. I would have crumpled in a heap there and then if I hadn't noticed Mum's door standing wide open. Pat spotted it, too, and gave me a worried look. I gave her the pram and hurried over, scared to death at what I might find inside.

I could hear crying and went in to find Mum in the kitchen, her head in her hands. I said, 'Are you all right? Did he hurt you?' and she looked up at me with mascara-streaked cheeks and said, 'What have I done, Bianca? What have I done?' I could see how much she was suffering and said, 'It's all right. I'm gonna be here. I'm not going to Manchester, I've cancelled my course.' I decided this morning that was the only way I could begin to right the wrongs I've committed. I showed Mum the letter, to prove it to her, and she told me I'd be throw-ing away my future and end up just like her. I said, 'If you'll forgive me, that's all I want.' As far as I was concerned, if it meant getting her back it was an easy sacrifice to make.

She stared at me with bloodshot eyes, as if she was trying to see deep inside me, and I thought she was gonna say yes. Then her mouth set into a hard line and she said, 'I don't want you round here no more. I want you to go up to Manchester, get out of my face. You're not welcome here'. She swiped the letter out of my hand, ripped it up and threw the pieces at me. Her face was like thunder. She got up and started coming at me, her arm raised. I was five years old again and petrified. I backed away, knocking a chair, and she forced me out of the kitchen and into the hall. She said, 'Now go. Go!' and her voice was deadly. I was edging backwards out of the door, pleading with her to listen, but she pushed me outside and hissed, 'Tomorrow you get on that train and disappear. I don't ever want to see you again'. Then she slammed the door in my face.

I heard a noise and looked across the Square and saw Ricky outside the Vic. Our eyes met for a fleeting second, then he turned away with a look of disgust and went inside. There was no-one else around. I was completely on my own. I'd been getting the message loud and clear all day, but now I knew it was final. I had no choice. I had to leave Walford.

10 September

I packed my bags last night, when I got in from seeing Mum. Our big things went up to the house in a van a few days ago, when me and Ricky were still planning on moving up to Manchester together. Seems a lifetime ago, now. Frank came round this morning and told me to give it one last try with Ricky. Good old Frank, eh? He's always been pretty decent to me and I ain't exactly been an easy daughter-in-law. I didn't think Ricky would listen, not after all the things he's said, but Frank said Ricky still loved me but he was too stubborn to admit it.

I had a cab booked in twenty minutes to take me and Liam to the station, but Frank had given me hope that Ricky and

I could still turn things around. I put Liam in his pram and set off for the Arches. Natalie was heading away from the Arches as I approached. She looked like she was gonna cut me dead, but I started to speak to her and she had to stop. I told her I was sorry about lying to her and she said, 'That's the least of your crimes. 'Sides, it's your loss, not mine.' I said, 'We're still mates, though, ain't we?' and she looked me up and down and replied, 'I don't know, Bianca. I don't know if we ever were.' She said she'd see me around, but it was clear she didn't wanna have anything to do with me again. She walked off up the road, my last friend gone. I didn't have the energy to cry any more. I knew I'd abused her loyalty like I'd abused everyone else's. I didn't expect Nat to stick by me. Why would she? I wouldn't if I was her.

Frank was wrong. Ricky didn't want to see me. He was revving a car and I had to pull out the ignition keys just to get him to talk. He wasn't impressed to hear that I loved him and he didn't believe that I wanted to make it up to him. He said it wouldn't last and in six months time I'd have a whole load of trendy new friends from college and he wouldn't get a look-in. 'The fact is, I ain't what you want, never have been.' He thinks him and me only got together because everyone was on our case, telling us not to. I remember that, David, Carol, Pat, all trying to stop us, but it wasn't that what attracted me to Ricky. I thought he was sexy and sweet and I really wanted him. I tried to tell Ricky that, how sleeping in David's old room at Pat's had brought back memories of when we sneaked back there and first made love. Ricky turned away and brushed his eyes and I said, 'Ricky, don't cry, I love you. If I ain't got you, I ain't got anything.' But it was all in vain. He said, 'No, I can't. It's too much. We just gotta forget it all, put it behind us and start again.' He told me to go, and when I wouldn't, he did.

After that, I thought I might as well cut my losses and go round to Mum's. I'd had two final rejections in the space of a few minutes, might as well go for the hat trick. I wasn't expecting her to welcome me with open arms, but I had to say goodbye, whatever she thought of me. And she certainly didn't hold back from telling me that all over again. She was as bitter and cutting as before and flatly refused to forgive me. I tried to hug her goodbye, but she stood as stiff as a board and wouldn't hold me. Sonia and Robbie came round a bit and said goodbye, but Mum refused to even come to the door.

I thought that was it, and went back to Pat's, where the cab was waiting. Pat had loaded my bags and we hugged and I thanked her for everything. I was getting into the back when someone called my name. I turned, and there was Mum. She came up to me and said, 'What's wrong with me? I can't even hate you properly'. I was so overcome I just fell into her arms, and this time she pulled me close. She said, 'You're my daughter. Nothing's gonna change that.' I said, 'Let me stay then. Let me look after you,' but she told me I had a new life to go to. I confessed how scared I was and she said, 'I know. So am I.' That made me realize, however tough my future was gonna be, Mum's was gonna be just as tough, if not tougher. I knew she was letting me go so that I could have something she'd never had, and I loved her for it with all my heart.

Sonia saw me to the station and helped with Liam and the bags, then I told her to go. I was on the concourse and heading for the platform when I ran into Dan – literally. I was searching for my ticket and not looking where I was going and he must have stepped out in front of me. He was a sight, all rough and unshaven and in a crumpled shirt and suit, and his breath smelt of drink.

I was shocked, a bit frightened even after what he did to Liam, especially when he said he was coming with me. He said, 'I didn't want all this to happen, but now it has, there's nothing to stop us. We can be together, go to Manchester...' I thought he'd flipped or something. I couldn't believe he was saying that after all that had happened. He was completely deluding himself. I said, 'Listen to me, it weren't never gonna work, it was a mess from the start.' But he wouldn't listen. He said he loved me and I loved him. I told him I was wrong and he tried to coax me, but it didn't work this time. He stroked my cheek with his fingers and I felt nothing. Once I would have shivered with excitement, but now – now he was some sad, seedy, middle-aged loser whose touch revolted me.

I stood my ground and said, 'Dan, it's over. All of it,' and he started to fall apart. He was crying, 'No, it can't be, it can't just evaporate.' He begged me, said he couldn't go back to how things were before, he needed me – everything I'd wanted to hear him say before. Now it fell on deaf ears. He was clutching at my arm, trying to stop me, but I told him to leave me alone. I warned him, 'Don't make me shout at you, upset Liam. Go away. Go away. Go away.' I kept repeating it at him 'til finally he got the message and let go. I turned around and quickly walked away with Liam, glad that I would never, ever see Dan's face again.

The train was in and a kind woman helped me load the pushchair on to it. I parked Liam in the corridor while I piled the bags in and was just about to board the train myself when I heard Ricky's voice shouting my name. I turned round and there he was, running up the platform towards me. He was panting and gasping so much, he could hardly speak. I screamed, 'Ricky!' and threw my arms around him and covered his face with kisses. I was so happy he'd come. I thought everything would be all right now.

I said, 'Oh look at you, you're gorgeous. You're mine, aren't you? You're all mine.' He pulled away and looked into my eyes and asked, 'Am I?' I told him I loved him, that he'd saved my life. Then the guard blew the whistle and started slamming doors. I wanted us both to get on, but Ricky hung back. My mouth went dry. I said, 'You are coming, aren't you?', but he wouldn't move. He asked if I really wanted him to and when I said yes he suddenly launched into this speech about how much he loved me.

The train was about to go and I was desperate for Ricky to get on, but he said he had a question and he wanted me to be honest. He said, 'I need to know that you feel the same as me. That you love me the same. That I ain't second best, that I'm enough for you, cos that's all I want. I ain't interested in anyone else. Is that how you feel about me?'

I laughed and said, 'Yes, of course, you idiot', but his face was dead serious. He went, 'Bianca, this isn't a joke. This is the rest of my life I'm talking about. I want you to be honest. If you love me, you'll be honest. In your heart, do you really believe I'm enough for you? Do you feel the same?'

The train started to crawl forwards and I panicked, cos Liam was on it, then it jolted and stopped. I was terrified of letting it go without us, and almost as terrified of saying the wrong thing and stopping Ricky from coming with us. He was standing still, waiting for an answer, so I smiled and held out my hand and said, 'I love you. You're my little darlin', you're my best friend.' He went, 'Is that the same?' and there was something different about his face, something I'd never seen in it before. He looked ... like a grown-up.

I know that sounds silly, but I've always seen Ricky as a boy. Dan was big, hunky, masculine, all man – to look at, anyway. Too late I found out that inside, he was just an immature boy who wanted toys he couldn't have. But Ricky – Ricky was a kid when I met him and that's how I've always thought of him. I don't think I've ever really let him grow up in my mind. Then, today, on the platform, I could see it. Ricky had changed. He wasn't a funny, bumbling, earnest duffer, he was a grown man, a responsible man, and he was taking charge of something that I didn't have the willpower or the self-control to do. He was laying himself open in front of me and asking me to do the same. Absolute honesty. I knew I owed him that much, what-ever I wanted from him. And I wanted him with me so badly … I was so torn. But I'd told him so many lies for so long. I'd been lying to him from the start. And to myself. It was time for that to stop.

'Is it the same?' I met Ricky's eyes. We held the moment. I took a deep breath, and said, 'No. I'm sorry.' He looked shaken and said, 'That's all I wanted to know'. I told him he could still come with us, but he turned and walked away, shouting, 'I'll call you,' over his shoulder.

The train was creeping forwards. I had to get on. I slammed the door shut and leaned out of the window. Ricky was still walking down the platform. I shouted his name and he stopped and turned round. I smiled at him, trying to tell him it would be alright. He smiled back. Not a big smile – just a little smile. But it told me enough. It told me that Ricky and I would still be there for each other, not as lovers, but as Liam's parents. It wouldn't be easy, but we'd manage it. We'd still be a family, of sorts. Miles apart in distance, but not so very far apart as friends. It was something to hold on to. I took Liam in my arms and hugged him tight. The train pulled out of the station. There was no going back.

CAST MEMBERS WHO APPEAR
IN THE PHOTOGRAPHS

Bianca Butcher (nee Jackson) — Patsy Palmer

Carol Jackson — Lindsey Coulsen

Alan Jackson — Howard Antony

Robbie Jackson — Dean Gaffney

Sonia Jackson — Natalie Cassidy

Billy Jackson — Devon Anderson

David Wicks — Michael French

Joe Wicks — Paul Nicholls

Tiffany Mitchell (nee Raymond) — Martine McCutcheon

Natalie Price — Lucy Speed

Ricky Butcher — Sid Owen

Dan Sullivan — Craig Fairbrass

THE AUTHOR

Kate Lock was born in Oxford, where she grew up and began her career as a journalist on the *Oxford Star*. She moved to London, where she worked for *Radio Times* for six years, and continues to write for the magazine as a freelance. She has written five other novelisations: Jimmy McGovern's *The Lakes* (as K. M. Lock) for BBC/Penguin; *Where the Heart Is: Home* and *Where the Heart Is: Relative Values* (Headline) and *Blood Ties: The Life and Loves of Grant Mitchell* (BBC) and *Tiffany's Secret Diary* (BBC), which became a number one bestseller. She now lives in York with her husband, Stephen, and daughter, Isis.

EastEnders

Publishing available:

VIDEO
The Mitchells: Naked Truths
Phil and Grant remember the laughs, the tears and the fights
– And settle some old scores...
Starring Ross Kemp, Steve McFadden and
Barbara Windsor.
BBCV 6623/£13.99

BOOKS
Blood Ties: The Life and Loves of Grant Mitchell
by Kate Lock
Chronicling the vibrant and colourful life story of Grant
Mitchell – EastEnders' favourite rogue.
ISBN 0 563 38483 2 / £4.99

Tiffany's Secret Diary
by Kate Lock
Follow Tiffany's turbulent years on the square with
her secret diary.
ISBN 0 563 55104 6 / £4.99

Available now from all good retailers